Rwanda

Which Way Now?

A. HOLLMANN/UNHCR

Contents

Oxfam (UK and Ireland) **David Waller**

FRANCES RUBIN/OXFAM

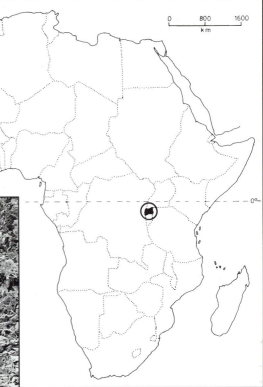

VINCENT BANABAKINTU/OXFAM

Above left: **volcano in the Virunga National Park**
Above: **map of Africa, showing position of Rwanda**
Left: **gorillas in north-west Rwanda**
Below: **on the shores of Lake Kivu**

WHITNEY GARBERSON/OXFAM

The land of a thousand hills

I F YOU THINK OF AFRICA — as many people do — as a flat, brown, sandy land with few trees and little rain, Rwanda comes as a shock to the senses. With lush green slopes enfolding much of the country, it is often called 'the Land of a Thousand Hills'. Although it is just one degree south of the Equator, its high altitude produces average annual temperatures of 19°C and regular rainfall (averaging 85 mm each month) that support a wide range of crops, grown on every available inch of land.

Rwanda is in the centre of Africa, on the watershed between the Nile and Zaire river basins. Most of the country is more than 1,500 metres above sea-level. It has tropical rainforest at the higher and wetter altitudes in the west, which gradually changes to lower and thinner scrub in the south and east. The highest slopes of the Virunga volcanic mountains in the north-west of Rwanda are one of the last refuges of the mountain gorillas, made famous by the film *Gorillas in the Mist* about the life and death of the North American naturalist, Dian Fossey. In the east the Akagera National Park is home to wild life as varied as that found in the better-known game parks of Kenya and Tanzania. Ten per cent of Rwanda's area is protected, either as National Parks or as Forest Reserves — considerably more than most other African countries.

Appearances are deceptive if you arrive at Kigali's modern and efficient airport, and drive along the well-maintained roads past newly completed office blocks and the Parliament building. Even on leaving the capital for the rural areas, you see such ordered and verdant fertility that it is difficult to believe that Rwanda could possibly suffer from environmental problems, that people could go hungry and be malnourished, that communities could live in an abject poverty from which there is no obvious means of escape. And yet they do. Why? And what are the prospects for the future?

The answers to these questions are not simple. They are buried in the country's long history, in the interaction of local, regional, and international forces which need to be understood individually before they can make sense collectively.

Imana yirirwa ahandi igataha i Rwanda —
God spends the day elsewhere, but always comes back to spend the night in Rwanda.
(Rwandan proverb)

Above: **azaleas at the edge of Lake Kivu**

Below: **Rainforest and river in north-west Rwanda**

VINCENT BANABAKINTU/OXFAM

The roots of conflict

Batwa, Bahutu, and Batutsi

Between 2000 BC and 1000 AD, people migrated in successive waves into the area between the Rift Valley lakes of Central Africa. These pygmoid people lived by hunting and gathering in the forests. Their descendants, who are still hunter-gatherers, are known as **Batwa**. They now form less than one per cent of the total population of Rwanda.

For the next 500 years new people migrated into the area. They concentrated on clearing the land for cultivation. Their society was organised in small monarchies, based on clans of related families. Their social and cultural life was geared to preserving and promoting the interests of these clans and their alliances. This population of cultivators is often presumed to be **Bahutu**, who now form almost 90 per cent of the population.

Then, between the sixteenth and nineteenth centuries AD, a taller group of people known as the **Batutsi** emerged as the dominant military and economic force.

It was they who introduced the lyre-horned Ankole cattle into Rwanda. They reinforced their military strength by developing an oral mythology which taught that the Batutsis' dominance over the Bahutu and Batwa was ordained by God, and that the Batutsi and their Mwami (king) were omnipotent in all walks of life. Even though they were a minority in society, the Batutsi controlled all areas of the country, except the north and west, by means of a complicated administrative system. Bahutu were tied to their Batutsi chiefs by a system of 'clientage' in which the Mututsi patron could deny his Muhutu client access to pasture, or to cattle, or to military protection, if the client did not provide free labour and a proportion of his crops to the patron.

The Batutsi Mwamis also manipulated a complex web of spies, and thus not only maintained their power, but developed a capacity for political intrigue and paranoia that remains to this day throughout Rwandan society.

Lyre-horned cattle in Gikoro Commune

VINCENT BANABAKINTU/OXFAM

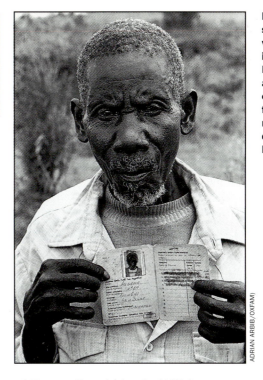

In the Kinyarwanda language, **Ba-** is a noun prefix that signifies 'people'. Thus Twa people are called Batwa. The singular form is **Mu-**, as in Mutwa.

The uses of history

This summary of Rwanda's pre-colonial history, although widely accepted, is rather too neat and uncontroversial. History in Rwanda, as in any society, is used to serve the particular ends of those who are telling it.

There are differences of perception, and the most important relates to the question of who exactly the Batutsi are, and the precise nature of their relationship to the Bahutu. Did they dominate them in a semi-feudal hierarchy of master and serf, or was their relationship mutually beneficial? Ever since aristocratic German explorers first pronounced the Batutsi to be an elite of nilo-hamitic origins, the Bahutu and the Batutsi have been regarded as separate ethnic groups. But some authorities now suggest that the differences between all three 'ethnic' groups result from social differentiation within the clan system, and not from the successive waves of immigration of different groups. The evidence from archaeological, linguistic, and comparative sources is inconclusive, and each group tends to believe the theory that suits its interests best.

Although it will be hard to establish an objective version of history, endorsed by all ethnic groups, in the end it will be essential to work out a truly national and non-sectarian interpretation of Rwanda's past, if the current wounds of ethnic conflict are to be healed.

Germans, French, and Belgians

The first European explorers arrived in Rwanda in 1894. In the same year the European powers, meeting at the Congress of Berlin, divided Africa among themselves. Rwanda, along with Urundi, now Burundi, was declared to form part

Identity cards, still in use today, were first introduced by the Belgian colonial authorities. Their effect was to formalise and reinforce ethnic divisions within Rwandan society.

ADRIAN ARBIB/OXFAM)

of German East Africa. In 1897 the Rwandan Mwami agreed to his country becoming a German protectorate, even though the only enemies around were Belgium and Britain — who were of concern to the Germans, rather than to the Rwandans. The Germans imposed Batutsi chiefs on the north of the country.

Two years later the first French Catholic missionaries arrived from Uganda (where they had been the ultimate losers of three successive religious wars). Within a few years they had set up six missions placed strategically around the country. The Catholic church fully accepted the racially-based interpretation of society that regarded the Batutsi as inherently superior to the Bahutu. The missionaries lent their weight to the idea, and ensured that it was continued when the Belgians took over from the Germans.[1]

In 1911 resentment against the Germans, the Batutsi chiefs, and the Catholic Church led to a short-lived popular uprising in the north of Rwanda, near Ruhengeri. It was crushed militarily, but left continuing bitterness among northerners towards those whom they considered outsiders, and in particular towards the Batutsi.

Muyaneza's story

In 1960, Muyaneza, a Muhutu peasant, told his life story to a researcher,[2] who recorded that the old man had been a vassal to three Batutsi 'overlords' in the course of his life. The first one had allowed him the use of two cows in return for labour. But, after five years of service, Muyaneza fell foul of his master's mother: she ordered him to give his sister as a concubine to her son; Muyaneza refused, and the master's mother took back the two cows. ... The second overlord allowed Muyaneza to use more cows, but took them all back when he decided to leave the country. ... By the time Muyaneza had found a third overlord, his wife and mother had died, leaving him to care for his children alone; moreover, he himself was ill. But Sesonga, the master, made no allowances for Muyaneza's misfortunes, and pursued him relentlessly for what was due to him under the traditional system of clientage. Many thousands of Bahutu peasants were similarly vulnerable to exploitation as vassals of Batutsi masters.

During the First World War the German forces in Rwanda, defeated by the Belgians, were expelled. Although the Belgians took over Rwanda under a League of Nations Mandate, they continued the German policy of indirect administration (partly because it was cheap) and reinforced ethnic divisions within the population still further. Bahutu were removed from all positions of authority within society, and blocked from all higher education except training for the priesthood. Constrained by the demands of their colonial masters, Batutsi chiefs used their powers within the traditional and colonial systems so that the old system which ensured mutual benefits gave way to outright exploitation and repression: Bahutu peasants who had given labour and support to their patrons in return for access to cattle, pasture, and security now provided it just because they had to, with no expectation of receiving anything in return.

Having used the system of indirect rule for their own ends, the colonial authorities were inadvertently destroying the legitimacy of the rule of traditional authorities among the population.

Reversals and revolution

With the creation of the United Nations in 1945, Rwanda-Urundi was designated as a Belgian 'Trustee Territory'. The UN insisted on plans for national independence and on the introduction of elected advisory structures. In the 1950s the Catholic Church and the Belgian administration, after years of favouring the Batutsi in education and employment and using them to administer the country on their behalf, abruptly switched their allegiance from them to the Bahutu, and tried to push through reforms.

There were several reasons for this change of policy. A new generation of colonial and church leaders, many of whom had fought against ethnic elitism in Europe in the Second World War, were uncomfortable with the feeling that their organisations were sustaining similar racist policies in Rwanda. And as the world polarised around the two great super-powers of the Cold War, and the 'winds of change' began to sweep throughout Africa, the Batutsi were perceived to be supporting ideas of radical pan-africanism that were seen as a threat to Western interests. So the church and the administration were only too keen to accept the 'democratic' and pliant alternative offered by the emerging Bahutu elite.

In 1959 Bahutu leaders insisted on fundamental change, and the Batutsi leaders resisted. There was tension and then violence, aimed initially against the Batutsi chiefs and then progressively against the wider Batutsi population. With

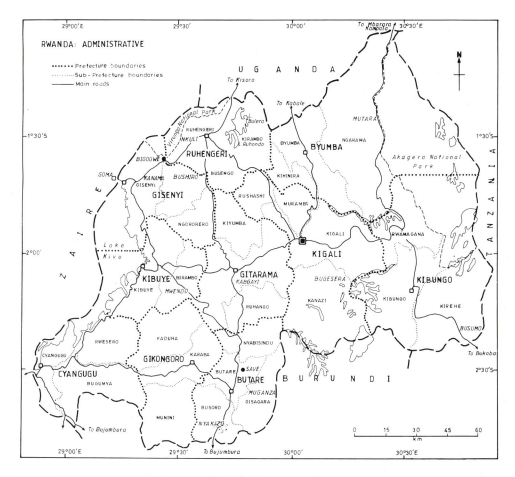

RWANDA: ADMINISTRATIVE

••••• Prefecture boundaries
······ Sub-Prefecture boundaries
——— Main roads

Belgian support, more than half of the Batutsi chiefs and sub-chiefs were replaced by Bahutu within the space of a few months. Between 1960 and 1962 the violence spread: 10,000 Batutsi were killed, and another 120,000 fled to neighbouring countries as refugees. Many remain there to this day.[3]

In 1961 the monarchy was abolished by a constitutional *coup d'état* mounted by the newly empowered Bahutu elite, with the support of the Belgian authorities. The population voted for independence, which was granted on 1 July 1962. The UN Trust Territory became two separate states: the Republic of Rwanda and the Kingdom of Burundi. But (as with many revolutions) the Rwandan Revolution was rather the start of a process of change than the end.

Marc's story

No catalogue of dates can tell us how Rwanda's history was lived by its citizens. One of those whose life was frequently affected by that history was Marc, a Mututsi, born in 1943 in Kibuye.

Marc's father, who owned about 50 cattle, worked as a clerk in the sub-chief's office. In November 1959, when the Revolution started, the Bahutu population staged an angry demonstration. The Mututsi sub-chief was thrown out and replaced by a Muhutu. (He would have been killed if it hadn't been for friends, both Bahutu and Batutsi, who helped him to escape.)

In July 1960 rumours reached Kibuye of fighting between Bahutu and Batutsi in Gikongoro and Kigali; many Batutsi civilians had been killed and their houses were burnt down. One night all Marc's cattle were killed by having their legs cut off. When the new sub-chief made it clear that he was not going to do anything about it, the family fled to Butare — never to return. ...

Independence and after

The First Republic, 1962-73

The hatred between Bahutu and Batutsi left by the violent overthrow of the traditional system of government was kept alive between 1961 and 1967 by the numerous attacks led by Batutsi refugees based in Uganda and Burundi; these fighters were known as the 'Inyenzi' (the 'cockroaches'). The Bahutu majority in Rwanda feared that if these attacks were successful, they would once again be subjugated by the Batutsi minority. Events in Burundi, where the Batutsi remained in power, justified that fear in the minds of many Rwandans.

People in the north of Rwanda, particularly in Ruhengeri and Gisenyi, resented the economic advantages gained by President Kayibanda's home region of Gitarama and the influence (as they saw it) of Batutsi within the country — despite the fact that the government was overwhelmingly Bahutu in its make-up. After 1967, when the external threat from the Inyenzi receded, the tension between north and south and between Bahutu and Batutsi people increased.

In 1972, following widespread ethnically motivated killings of Bahutu in neighbouring Burundi, there were violent reprisals in Rwandan schools: many Batutsi were killed, or barred from continuing their education. There is a widespread suspicion among Rwandans that these incidents were orchestrated by the army chief of staff, Juvenal Habyarimana, to create the conditions for his *coup d'état* in July 1973. Habyarimana became President, and power effectively moved from Gitarama to his home area of Bushiru in Gisenyi. Whether or not the suspicions are well-founded, they add to the mistrust between Habyarimana and the opposition parties.

Marc's story cont'd

... In the years that followed the Revolution, Marc and his family often feared for their lives as tension rose between the Batutsi and the Bahutu populations. In 1973 Marc's younger brother was expelled from secondary school — simply for being Mututsi. Marc decided to go to Burundi to see if the situation would be better there. To his surprise, the Batutsi in power there were suspicious of their Rwandan brothers, and after six years of exile, when things had calmed down in Rwanda, he returned to Butare. ...

The Second Republic, 1973 to 1991

President Habyarimana took power with the declared aim of creating national unity. The ministers of the First Republic were killed, and President Kayibanda was kept under house arrest until he died in 1975.

In 1975 the National Revolutionary Movement for Development (MRND) was created and all other parties banned. A quota system was introduced, with the aim of ensuring that all ethnic groups and regions were treated fairly in education and employment. The education system was reformed, and the government introduced the practice of *umuganda*: a system of community labour on buildings, tree-planting and anti-erosion activities, and road maintenance. Rwanda and Burundi adopted a policy of 'good neighbourliness', promising not to interfere in each other's affairs. This co-operation was consolidated by the creation of the 'Economic Community of the Great Lakes Countries', the CEPGL, which brought Rwanda, Burundi, and Zaire together in a structure which was supposed to encourage regional development.

For the average Rwandan citizen, politics in Rwanda's one-party state consisted mostly of singing the praises of the President in the weekly 'animation' sessions, and the occasional rumour of conflict within the ruling elite. Elections were held in 1981, 1985, and 1989. President Habyarimana made sure that he always won with more than 90 per cent of the vote. (In 1989 there was even a campaign to have him elected by 100 per cent of the electorate!) Only two Tutsi candidates were allowed to stand for election to the national assembly in the following year; both won seats.

The achievements of Independence ...

In 1987 there were great official celebrations of the first 25 years of Independence — but what in fact had been achieved?

The government could point to many creditable achievements. Its pragmatic policies and the generally well-managed economy of Rwanda had been rewarded by an influx of aid money (averaging more than $200 million per year). The money had been visibly put to use: the road network had been transformed, so that all prefectures except Kibuye were linked by asphalted roads; water systems had been put in place, so that almost 70 per cent of the rural population had access to safe drinking water;[4] offices had been built at national, prefectoral, and communal levels; the housing of the average peasant had been improved; a peasants' bank had been created, with over 100 branches 'on the hills'; the electricity and telephone networks had been extended, and a fleet of buses provided to link all the prefectures and sub-prefectures on a daily basis; and the government civil service had been enlarged, trained, and equipped, with officials who were better paid than any others in the region.

Umuganda: until recently, citizens contributed one day's labour each week to community projects

More exciting than these merely material creations was the change in attitudes that was occurring among the rural population. Rwanda, like many colonised countries concerned with exporting its crops, had long had a formal co-operative sector, but it was the emergence of thousands of informal associations during the Second Republic that was really new. As the associations came together in ever larger federations, their potential political power became apparent. Although the advent of multi-party politics has led to the federations' leaders being manipulated by the parties for their own sectarian ends, there are signs that the dynamic of peasant farmers asserting their rights against the urban elite is still alive. If it is, it will be one of the most important outcomes of the Second Republic.

... and the legacy of ethnic conflict

In retrospect it is possible to see that the slow changes that were occurring in Rwandan society, although important, were not enough to fend off the tidal wave of problems that was about to crash upon the country. In 1989 there was a famine that affected much of the south-west; there was growing discontent about corruption among the country's political elite (discontent which was being fuelled by an emerging independent press); and during

9

1990 the pressure to solve the problem of Rwandan refugees still living in surrounding countries, and to radically restructure the economic and political systems, became ever greater.

But the government was hemmed in on all sides: by a history of mistrust that was particularly marked between the northerners who monopolised power within the country and the Batutsi outside the country who were demanding their right to return; by the inertia produced by 17 years in power without an effective opposition to stimulate debate on policy questions; by the lack of easy solutions to the country's problems; and by Rwanda's growing dependence on its foreign funders — who, inspired by events in Eastern Europe, were increasingly insistent on political change. The government responded to Rwanda's problems by doing too little, too late.

The Batutsi refugee community in Uganda was very powerful: many of its young men had fought alongside Yoweri Museveni in Uganda's war of independence between 1981 and 1986, and Museveni's Deputy Minister of Defence, Fred Rwigyema, was just one of many Rwandan refugees who held key military and political positions. There was a real threat that these hardened soldiers might try to fight their way home to Rwanda, so in 1988 negotiations were opened between the Rwandan and Ugandan governments to try to solve the refugee problem.

Although progress was made on technical issues, it was more difficult to agree on the political reforms that were needed to make a return of refugees possible. In July 1990, having flatly refused a move to political pluralism just two months earlier, the President announced that multi-party politics would be introduced and that the Party and the State would be separated. Many refugees in Uganda, refusing to believe that the move was genuine, decided that further negotiations were pointless.

Marc's story cont'd

... For Marc the political history of Rwanda was less important than the AIDS epidemic that came to affect him and his family.

When he returned to Rwanda from his fruitless search for work in Burundi, Marc discovered that jobs in the civil service were closed to him, because he was a Mututsi. Instead he was lucky to find work with an international organisation based in Kigali. Marc left his family in Butare, and would visit them for the weekend every few months.

In 1984 a thief tried to enter his lodgings in Kigali, and when Marc tried to stop him, the thief attacked with a machete and almost cut his arm off. In hospital Marc was given a blood transfusion and soon recovered, although he was never again able to do heavy work.

1988 was a bad year. Marc fell ill first with malaria, then with tuberculosis, and then with bacterial meningitis. At one time it looked as if he would die, but after almost a year he seemed to have recovered, and he eventually returned to work. Meanwhile his three-year-old daughter was scalded to death when she fell on to the fire at home in Butare and knocked over a pot of boiling water. ...

Rwanda under siege

ON 1 OCTOBER 1990 4,000 Batutsi refugees, deserters from President Museveni's army in Uganda, attacked northern Rwanda from their base over the border. Calling themselves the Rwandan Patriotic Front, they were led by Fred Rwigyema. The rebels declared that the political reform process was inadequate and that President Habyarimana must go. Although their sophisticated political analysis of the problems facing Rwanda was widely seen as correct, most people in Rwanda believed that the real reason behind the attack was far simpler: namely an attempt to take over the government of the country.

After spectacular successes during the first week of the war, the RPF met resistance from government troops, aided by France, Belgium, and Zaire. The war turned into a protracted guerrilla conflict. Between November 1990 and July 1992 the rebels gradually took a strip of land along a length of Rwanda's border with Uganda. Life for ordinary people became dominated by news of arrests and sectarian killings; the tension was increased by all-night curfews, and the search for papers to authorise residence, identity, and travel. Society was being gradually militarised, and polarised between the racial groups and between northerners and southerners. The horizons of life shrank to acute anxiety about what would happen during the next 24 hours.

A ceasefire was negotiated in Arusha, Tanzania, in July1992, but the subsequent 'Arusha negotiations' dragged on interminably as the parties comprising the fragile coalition government argued among themselves. When power-sharing arrangements were finally agreed in January 1993, the extremist Bahutu Party,

the Comité pour la Defense de la République (the CDR), emerged without any cabinet posts, and, together with elements of the MRND, some of its members responded by killing political opponents and Batutsi in Gisenyi and Ruhengeri. As a result, in February, the RPF — now perhaps 12,000 strong — renewed its attacks and doubled its territory in three days.

1990: people made homeless by the Rwandan civil war took refuge in Kamwezi Camp, on the border with Uganda

TONY BURDON/OXFAM

11

The number of Rwandans displaced from their homes by the civil war leapt from 350,000 to 900,000 (12 per cent of the population). Peace talks were resumed, but the chances of a lasting settlement seem depressingly small.

At the same time that the war started, the government introduced its economic structural adjustment programme. The effect was a severe economic slow-down that affected all parts of the population — apart from the army (which grew from a force of about 5,000 men to around 35,000 in only two years). The World Bank estimated in 1992 that the war was costing Rwanda about US$100 million a year. The country's hesitant progress towards prosperity during the 1980s was obliterated by the new social and economic problems.

Multi-party politics — but is it democracy?

The war in Rwanda has had one welcome and unexpected effect. Political dissension, suppressed in the long period since Independence, is now out in the open. The gradual relaxation of political life at the end of the 1980s has led in war-time to a surge of new ideas and political activity, unknown since the years of revolution between 1959 and 1962.

Some of the supporters of multi-party politics expected it to bring cheaper education, more affordable health care, and an end to food shortages. They are almost certainly mistaken, given that political pluralism is gaining ground at the same time as the introduction of a programme of structural adjustment to new levels of poverty which include increased 'cost-sharing' (i.e. making the consumer pay more) for health, education, and agricultural advice.

The truth is that, whatever their political colour, none of the opposition parties has succeeded in creating a credible vision of Rwanda's future. Their analysis of the causes of Rwanda's problems is still very weak, and instead of developing policies necessary to remedy them, the newly emerged factions are concentrating on opposing the President and his party.

In April 1992 a transitional coalition government was formed, drawn from the five most prominent of Rwanda's political parties, and given the task of negotiating peace with the RPF and organising elections. A year later its mandate was

Rwanda: an up-date

One year after the Postscript to this book was written, the crisis in Rwanda has deepened still further. In a mere 80 days, the population grew by 1.5 million (from an estimated total of 6 million people in October 1996), as the huge refugee camps in eastern Zaire, and others in Tanzania, were emptied, and Hutus who had fled from Rwanda after the genocide of 1994 returned home.

The Rwandan government had tried in vain to persuade the Hutu refugees that it was safe to go back; but they were intimidated by rumours of the retribution which would greet them on their return, and forcibly prevented from leaving by the remnants of the former Rwandan army and the Interahamwe militia who controlled the camps. However, when Banyamulenge rebels living in eastern Zaire joined Laurent Kabila's Allied Democratic Forces for the Liberation of Congo Zaire (ADFL) in October 1996, the camps were attacked and the people in them were dispersed.

Challenges for Rwanda

Rwanda now faces a range of daunting challenges. Hundreds of thousands of returned refugees must be accommodated, with respect for their dignity and human rights. Those innocent of complicity in the genocide must be re-integrated into social and political life without arousing the hatred of the surviving Tutsi population. The government of national unity must establish a State structure which will ensure the prevalence of justice, peace, and the rule of law.

The hand-picked National Assembly is beginning to gain confidence to act as an independent body, but a multi-party political system is still a long way off. Meanwhile, many powerless members of the community, especially widows,

orphans, and old people, and recently returned refugees, can take no part in debates about the future of the country.

Restoring the rule of law

The lack of access for independent observers makes it difficult to assess the situation accurately, but there are persistent stories of revenge attacks on Hutu civilians by Tutsi civilians, and of violations perpetrated by the army: pillaging, kidnapping, summary executions, and even massacres. There are also stories of witnesses of the genocide being murdered by returning members of the former Rwandan army and the Interahamwe death squads. Property disputes between returned refugees and the Tutsi who had taken over their fields and houses are a particular problem. Somehow the government of Rwanda must open a dialogue with the returned refugees, and ensure peace and stability in a country from which the ideology of genocide has not been eradicated.

The process of restoring justice to Rwanda is very slow. The police force and the judiciary are being reconstructed, but there is still a shortage of qualified officials. The international criminal tribunal in Arusha, which is trying the alleged ringleaders of the genocide in 1994, is hampered by a lack of resources and a lack of co-operation from neighbouring states. Twenty-one people accused of masterminding or being involved in the genocide have been indicted by the Tribunal.

Rwanda's overcrowded prisons now hold more than 100,000 people, waiting in appalling conditions to be dealt with by the inadequate judicial system. The numbers increase as more and more returning refugees are arrested on suspicion of involvement in the genocide. Special courts have been set up to handle juvenile cases. At the beginning of 1997 a total of 1,569 children under the age of 18 were being held; none will be charged with the crime of genocide, but they risk prosecution for offences committed in connection with the massacres by Hutu extremists.

Social tensions

Rwanda remains a deeply divided society. Fear and suspicion are rife: the fear of the returning refugees that they will be denounced, rightly or wrongly, for complicity in the genocide; and the fear of the survivors of genocide that they will lose what they have gained since 1994, now that refugees are returning to reclaim their property. Traditional community structures have disintegrated, and the social institutions which gave people a sense of belonging to a community, such as churches and mosques and other places considered sacred, were almost all desecrated.

Most crucially, Rwanda needs at least 300,000 new houses, to replace those destroyed during the civil war, and to avert communal conflict based on property disputes. Constructing new houses would go a long way towards helping people to work together again and to reintegrate them into their former communities; but this would require large-scale funding from major external donors — who at present take the view that there is still too much insecurity to risk investing in long-term social development programmes. The international community, which was spending US$1 million a day to feed the refugees in the camps outside Rwanda, now gives no aid to support the returned refugees.

One particular source of tension is the rapid growth of urban centres. Returning refugees, many of whom spent their exile in foreign cities, have been attracted to towns which until recently had been small settlements with very few services. There is no social structure to sustain the rapid growth in urban populations, and most towns in Rwanda are now breeding grounds for crime and social unrest.

Economic challenges

Rwanda faces severe economic challenges: it must share its meagre resources with a rapidly expanded population; but its infrastructure is in ruins, and according to the Food and Agriculture Organisation there has been a 12 per cent drop in the production of staple food crops.

The mass repatriation of refugees in late 1996 and early 1997 has inevitably disrupted the government's planning: the authorities had anticipated a gradual return of up to 60,000 people each month, over a period of one year or more. Most of the recent returners have brought back some skills from exile, but the country's commercial and industrial base is too narrow, and the civil-service sector too overstaffed, to absorb them all.

Given the fact that Rwanda is still up to 85 per cent dependent on peasant agriculture for its sustenance, the problem of landlessness and unequal land-holdings will have to be addressed as a matter of urgency. A new resettlement policy has affirmed that all land belongs to the State, and that it is the duty of the State to distribute it fairly. But even if all the land in Rwanda were allocated equitably, there would not be enough for everyone. There is therefore a great need to develop an alternative economy. But, with its reputation for instability, it will not be easy for Rwanda to attract the foreign investment which it desperately needs in order to create the economic security which will help the nation to avert future communal conflict.

extended by three months, to allow negotiations with the RPF to be concluded in Arusha.

But despite the rhetoric of reform, the President's party still controls the army and the national radio, and many Rwandans doubt if it will willingly give up power when the time comes. Many thousands of people, mostly Batutsi, have been arrested or have 'disappeared', and political opponents and journalists continue to be harassed and intimidated.

Almost 500 members of the Bagogwe community, related to the Batutsis, were massacred by security forces in early 1991. Hundreds more Batutsis were killed by Bahutu civilians in Bugesera in March 1992, and in Gisenyi in January 1993 by members of the extremist Bahutu party, the CDR, and elements of the MRND. In March 1993 an international commission of enquiry[5] accused both the RPF and the Rwandan army of abuses of human rights, including rape, summary executions, abductions of civilians, and the looting of peasants' homes. Bombs have exploded in restaurants, mini-buses, and public buildings. Many political parties have formed youth wings, regarded by many as militias, which attack each other with impunity.

Western donors are beginning to insist on progress towards democratisation in the countries of the South which receive their aid. The donors tend to accept the existence of plural political parties as evidence of a commitment to 'democracy'. In the case of Rwanda, it would be tragic if the advent of multi-party politics merely inflamed the regional and ethnic divisions that have plagued it in the past.

Who rules Rwanda?

This struggle for political supremacy is a struggle for the privilege of trying to deal with the seemingly intractable problems of agriculture, health, education, and wealth-creation — problems that have been made worse by years of neglect, while attention and resources have been invested in fighting rather than building.

The irony is that as the different sides struggle for supremacy, much of Rwanda's sovereignty is now vested in the Paris Club of creditor nations, in the European Community, and in the World Bank, which together define the economic environment within which the victors will be allowed to operate. While the poor on both sides are taught to hate each other with a renewed passion, real power is increasingly passing to the institutions of the rich North, so the identity of the ultimate winner becomes less important.

A burnt-out bus on the road between Ruhengeri and Kigali marks the scene of a gun battle between RPF forces and the Rwandan army in February 1993

Marc's story: the end

... For three years following his return to work, Marc would have days when he would suddenly burst out in rashes all over his body, when he would be absent-minded and tired. His wife became ill and died of bacterial meningitis. In September 1991 Marc was admitted to hospital, desperately ill. The doctor diag-nosed AIDS, and said that nothing could be done for him. When he died, Marc's colleagues could not believe it was from AIDS, because they associated that with men who were 'sexual vagabonds'. They did not know about the blood transfusion which followed the attack in 1984, which was the probable cause.

Marc left behind his six children, two of whom were just starting secondary school, while the youngest was only eight years old. In the midst of Rwanda's most acute political crisis since Independence, Marc died of a disease that knows nothing of ethnic differences or political power struggles, and causes horrible suffering and death indiscriminately. His story is a salutary reminder that when the civil war finally comes to an end, Rwanda's development problems, relegated to secondary importance since the start of the war, will have to be tackled — whoever the country's political leaders eventually turn out to be.

**AIDS poster at
the National
Information
Centre, Kigali**

FRANCES RUBIN/OXFAM

Exporting people and importing problems

Refugees: unfinished business

Ever since the Revolution of 1959-62 caused the flight of thousands of Batutsi into neighbouring countries, the question of their eventual return has been of paramount political importance. Their return posed severe political problems for the Bahutu government, which, until 1988, chose to ignore the question rather than deal with it.

There are now at least two million Banyarwanda who do not live in Rwanda. Some found themselves living in Uganda or Zaire when Rwanda's boundaries were re-drawn by the colonial powers in 1910; some left as 'economic migrants' during the last 90 years, often encouraged or coerced to move by the colonial authorities; and about 550,000[6] are recognised by the UN High Commissioner for Refugees as political refugees with the right to return to their country of origin.

One major reason why some of the refugees want to return to Rwanda is that they risk being treated as scapegoats when times are bad, despite their often positive contribution to the economic and social life of their host communities. In 1982, for example, Banyarwanda throughout Uganda were viciously persecuted, and many fled back to Rwanda until the situation in Uganda became less dangerous.

The war between the government and the Rwandan Patriotic Front that began in October 1990 has caused at least 25,000 more people, mostly Batutsi, to flee as refugees to surrounding countries. The problem of the refugees is now acute and demands a resolution. During ceasefire negotiations mediated by Rwanda's neighbours in March 1991, the Rwandan government for the first time fully recognised the right of Rwandan refugees to return home. But if they are to be repatriated, where will they live and how will they support themselves, in a country that is already desperately short of land for its present citizens? This question must be resolved before Rwanda, and indeed the entire region, can move on to tackle other important issues.

When pastoralists lose their homes, their cattle are displaced too: more than 40,000 cows were driven out of Uganda when their owners were expelled in 1982

N. VAN PRAAG/UNHCR

15

Félicien's story

The story of Félicien, a young Mututsi, reveals some of the problems of life as a refugee. Excluded from secondary school for being Mututsi, Félicien was sent by his mother to live with his aunt and attend school in Goma, just across the border in Zaire. Returning to Rwanda after completing his studies, he found work in Ruhengeri — where he was made to feel distinctly unwelcome.

In October 1990, three days after the war broke out, Félicien was arrested and accused of supporting the RPF. He was imprisoned in Ruhengeri, but was freed four months later, when rebel forces over-ran the town and liberated the prisoners. He escaped from the region by climbing over the volcanoes and crossing into Uganda. There the RPF tried to recruit him and other released prisoners. Félicien refused, not convinced that war was the way to solve Rwanda's problems.

Eventually he found work in Kampala, but the RPF still pressed him to join them, and several times he was threatened by members of the Ugandan security forces, who sympathised with the RPF. At the same time, the Rwandan embassy refused to help him, because he was Mututsi and had 'escaped' from prison. He was mistrusted by the community of refugees already established in Kampala, because his knowledge of Rwanda was more recent and less easily assimilated into their simplistic rhetoric.

'Those who have not lived in Rwanda recently believe that absolutely everything there is terrible,' Félicien says, 'and the Rwandan authorities assume that if you are Mututsi, you must be against them, and are therefore "guilty". All I want to do is get right out of this region, and leave the whole mess behind.'

Nyacyonga Camp, 15 km from Kigali: 80,000 people, displaced by the civil war, settled here in February 1993, laying bare a hillside once covered in trees

PAUL SHERLOCK/OXFAM

1988: a refugee problem in reverse — victims of ethnic violence in Burundi took refuge in Saga Camp, Rwanda

Rwanda in a regional context

Rwanda's problems cannot be understood in isolation from its relationship with the rest of the Great Lakes region. This relationship has several dimensions.

First, the pressure on land in Rwanda is so great that even more people are likely to migrate in desperation. But neighbouring countries are also under economic stress, and people there are likely to resent further immigration from Rwanda, and even the presence of existing immigrants. Rwandan migrants were expelled from Tanzania in 1990, and 1,000 were killed in communal violence in Zaire in April 1993.

Second, Rwanda's landlocked position, 1,500 km by road from the nearest port, makes it dependent on its neighbours for contacts with the outside world. The road and rail routes to the Indian Ocean ports of Mombasa in Kenya (via Uganda) and Dar es Salaam in Tanzania are lifelines for Rwanda. At various times in the past 20 years the upheavals in Uganda, and the military successes of the RPF on the border, have cut supply routes through Uganda.

The third dimension of Rwanda's regional position is the case of its relations with Burundi. Although much of the two countries' history is shared, and their populations are composed of almost identical proportions of Batwa, Bahutu, and Batutsi, in Burundi it is the Batutsi minority that still holds power, while in Rwanda the Bahutu majority are now dominant. Events in both countries have become inextricably linked as politics have become polarised along racial lines: each sees the hand of the other every time there are sectarian killings on either side of the border. As the political situation evolves in Burundi following elections in June 1993, events there will continue to affect (and be affected by) the instability in Rwanda.

Rwanda is a weak economy surrounded by other weak economies. Zaire, Tanzania, and Uganda all have natural resources, but for various reasons have not begun to fulfil their potential. Economic, demographic, and geographic logic would suggest closer co-operation between Rwanda and its neighbours, but the legacy of their colonial histories, their competing economies, and the suspicions born of conflict and poverty make this very unlikely in the immediate future. Until these problems are overcome, another possible solution to Rwanda's problems will remain out of reach.

Coventry University

17

Can Rwanda feed itself?

Population and land

With an area of over 26,000 sq km, Rwanda is about the same size as Wales or Belgium. The average population density in 1991 was 271 people per square kilometre — the highest in mainland Africa. (In Wales the comparable figure is 139, and in Belgium it is 322.) But if the lakes, National Parks, and Forest Reserves are excluded, the population density is far higher: the actual area of agricultural land (17,758 sq km) has to support an average of 422 people per square kilometre over the whole country. The most densely populated area is Ruhondo in Ruhengeri, with 820 people per sq km of usable land;

at the other end of the scale is Rusomo, Kibungo, with just 62 people per sq km of usable land.

Why does Rwanda have such a high density of population? One reason is that because of their effective military structures, Rwanda and Burundi were the only countries in central Africa to avoid the ravages of the Arab and European slave trades. Not only was Rwanda's population not reduced by the slave trade, but it actually increased as other people sought refuge there. Further settlement was encouraged by the local chiefs, because, under the 'clientage' system, the more clients a patron had, the

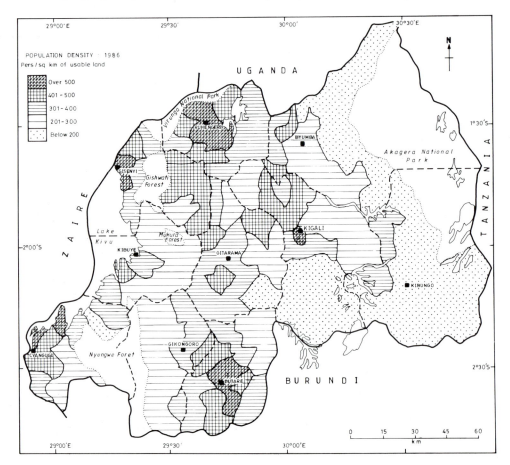

more powerful he became. None of this would have been possible if the soils and climate of the country had not been able to support the intensive cultivation practised in the area. Rwanda's temperate climate supports two and sometimes three seasons a year, which — combined with areas of fertile volcanic soils — give it a potential for agricultural production that is undreamed of in many other areas of Africa.

Rwanda's high population density has not been without its benefits. Since 1975 the government has tried to make use of its human resources through a system of community labour known as *umuganda*, under which all adults were supposed to give a day of work each week to community projects designated by the local authorities. This tax-in-the-form-of-labour has had valuable results: country lanes maintained, anti-erosion ditches and trenches for gravity-fed water systems dug, health centres and schools constructed, and vast areas of new forest planted. You only had to travel to neighbouring Zaire to see that without *umuganda* the state of the environment in general and the soils, forests, and roads in particular would have been far worse. But this system of taxation in kind has not been universally popular, nor always well managed. The advent of multi-party politics has brought an unofficial but widespread refusal to participate in *umuganda* unless it is for the direct benefit of the community. Thus, although communities still help with the building of schools and water systems, they are refusing to work on the maintenance of the roads that are used only by government officials and other members of the elite. So the future of the whole system is in doubt.

Nutrition in the balance

The emblem of the National Office of Population Activities, ONAPO, shows a pair of scales with people on one side, balanced by food on the other. The evidence of the past few years suggests that the balance is no longer being maintained. In 1984, the agricultural population of Rwanda numbered approximately 5.5 million. On average they each consumed 49 grammes of protein per day (the international recommended minimum is 59 grammes). By 1989, the agricultural population had risen to 6.5 million, but the average daily protein consumption was down to 36 grammes.[7]

These national figures conceal considerable seasonal and geographical variations: large areas of the country fail to produce enough food to support their populations. Figures produced by the Ministry of Agriculture[8] show that while in the seven years from 1966 to 1983 Rwanda increased its total production of

A Batwa farmer clearing a hillside for cultivation

SU HOPKINS/OXFAM

food by 4.3 per cent, in the five years from 1984 to 1989 production increased by only one per cent.

What are the reasons behind the current imbalance between population size and food production? The experience of two typical farmers explains some of the problems.

The story of Célestin and Odette

Twagiramungu Célestin and Akimabera Odette own a small plot of land (about half a hectare) in Gikongoro, which has poor acid soils. They have some avocado trees, some cassava, some bananas, and a few coffee plants that brought them an income of about 4,500 RWF (about £32.00) in 1989. They do not own any animals.[9]

Their situation has been getting worse since 1986. In 1989 erratic rains led to a general shortage of food. Célestin and his three-year-old son developed kwashiorkor, a form of malnutrition due to protein deficiency that causes limbs to swell, and leaves the sufferer lethargic and vulnerable to other diseases. Odette was overwhelmed by the heavy work of cultivating the fields, and the strain of

breast-feeding the youngest child, at a time when they went for several days at a stretch without eating.

In order to survive, the family sold half of their coffee plants, as well as the wood that bordered the edge of their plot. But the other people in the area were also suffering, so the prices they received were low and the money earned did not last long. They were reduced to eating the leaves of their cassava plants and beans, even though they knew this would reduce the yields at harvest time. They considered trying to steal someone else's crops, but had seen too many people beaten to death for having done so.

Célestin tried going to Burundi, 60 km away, to find work and food for his family. But, unlike previous years, so many people were competing for the same work that he could not bring back much food.

Odette tried working for neighbours in return for food, but their crops had also been affected by the erratic climate and new plant diseases, and they could not afford to pay others to do their work for them.

Their oldest son tried to get work at the Crete Zaire Nil project in Gikongoro, clearing degraded forestry and planting improved pastures and potatoes on the Nile-Zaire watershed. But here also, too many people were chasing too few jobs.

In 1990, better rains meant a bigger crop of beans and cassava, but the income from their coffee was reduced, partly because they had sold half the plants, but also because the price per kilo had fallen. In one week in 1989, the international price of coffee dropped by one-third. Célestin and Odette gave up hope of getting their children back into school. They no longer went to the health centre, because it had put up its charges for both consultations and medicines.

'Primitive' farming needs sophisticated decisions

The story of Célestin and Odette reveals some of the strategies that poor people use in order to survive in bad years. How do they manage their farms in normal years?

Breast-feeding and full-time farm work in times of food shortage put great strains on women's health

VINCENT BANABAKINTU/OXFAM

Farmers trekking through banana trees from one plot to another: the average peasant farm consists of at least five separate small plots of land

The most important aspect of Rwandan agriculture is its diversity and almost bewildering complexity. Deciding on the suitability of a given plot of land for a particular crop would already be complicated if the factors to be considered were only the rainfall, temperatures, soils, and slopes — which all vary extensively throughout the country. But these natural factors are dwarfed by the social and economic factors which individual farmers have to build into their decisions about what to plant and where.

The average Rwandan household farms at least five plots of land, which are scattered around at varying distances from the home, each with its own specific characteristics of fertility, accessibility, and form of tenancy. It is worth noting that 22 per cent of households are headed by women, and women are responsible for half of all decisions about what food crop to plant.

On the family's diverse plots the woman of the household must try to produce a constant supply of food throughout the year. Preferably the crops should be of more than one type, so that, for example, there is a carbohydrate-rich crop, such as potatoes, to complement a

protein-rich crop, such as beans. The family may also want a crop that will be harvested and sold at a time when they will need extra money to pay for items such as school fees or taxes.

In making his or her decisions, the farmer must also take into account the degree to which a particular crop requires fertile soils (beans and sorghum, for example) or can tolerate poor soils (like sweet potato), and the extent to which the crop either takes a lot out of the soil (like soy beans) or takes relatively little (like sweet potato). A recent study showed that, to preserve soil fertility, farmers in one small area in the south of the country grew 14 different crops in almost 50 different rotations.[10]

More than half the area under cultivation is intercropped: two and sometimes three different crops are planted together in the same field, because — although their individual performance varies according to the sequence and densities of planting — their combined productivity is up to 50 per cent greater than any one crop grown by itself.

Add to all this the further complications of trying to predict the market value of crops, and planning to minimise the effects of plant diseases and the danger of theft from fields (which increases with distance from the homestead), and you begin to get an idea of the sophistication of the decisions that the individual farmer must take to maximise the potential of his or her plots.

Shrinking farms ...

In Rwanda, land belongs to the State. In towns, where it is surveyed and registered, people can acquire the right of ownership. In rural areas, individuals only have rights to use land, not to own it. The State can reclaim the land for its own use, without compensation for the loss. The rights to use land can be sold (if the whole family endorses the contract), and they are passed down by inheritance from the father (who is legally the head of the household) to his sons.

In 1984 57 per cent of Rwandan households owned less than one hectare of land, and 25 per cent had less than one half hectare, from which they had to feed an average family of five people. (One hectare is almost 2.5 acres; a football pitch is approximately three-quarters of a hectare.) The inheritance laws, which

divide a family's land among all the remaining sons, ensure that, as the population increases, not only does the size of holdings fall, but they are increasingly fragmented into small plots, scattered over a wide area. The fact that the plots are scattered brings advantages as well as disadvantages, but their small total size makes it increasingly difficult to grow enough food for a family's needs.

It is tempting to suggest — as the National Commission for Agriculture has — that if land were consolidated into holdings of at least two hectares, it would be possible to introduce modern mechanised techniques that would increase overall productivity. But in Kenya, where a similar form of land consolidation was implemented during the 1950s, total production actually declined, because the different characteristics and requirements of the consolidated small plots were often ignored. And in Kenya (as elsewhere), attempts to redistribute land more fairly were compromised by political considerations, and many small farmers actually lost their land in the process.

Flood damage to banana trees in Nyamutera Commune

KAREN TWINING/OXFAM

... and declining soil fertility

Because of the small size of their holdings, farmers can no longer afford to let their land rest and recover through periods of fallow, as they used to. The plants go on extracting nutrients from the soil without a break, reducing its fertility. And the soil itself, with its nutrients, is leached away by rainfall as ever steeper slopes, with ever more fragile soils, are brought into production. Half of Rwanda's farming is done on slopes of more than 10 per cent; such slopes have tended to be abandoned in Europe, where agriculture has intensified on the flattest and most productive fields. On the steepest slopes, intense rainfall erodes more than 11 tonnes of soil per hectare per year, and a staggering 12 million tonnes of soil are exported by Rwanda's rivers each year.[11]

The Ministry of Agriculture and some of the international funding agencies, particularly the European Community, urge the use of chemical fertilisers to give a short-term boost to production. But others argue that imported chemical fertilisers are unsuitable, partly because they have to be paid for in scarce foreign currency, and partly because the soil is so lacking in humus (organic material) that it cannot absorb much of the chemical fertilisers anyway, with the result that they are rapidly leached away. As alternatives, some people propose increasing the combination of animal husbandry and cultivation in order to provide more manure. Others are trying to develop plants known as 'green fertilisers', which replenish rather then deplete the soils that they are grown in. Others maintain that ultimately it will be necessary to use some form of terracing to prevent the rainfall removing the farmers' most important item of capital, namely their soil and its fertility.

As yet there is no consensus about how to preserve the quality of Rwanda's soils. In the short term, agriculture in Rwanda will fail to be sustainable: each season, in order to survive, farmers aim for maximum yields, at the expense of the soil's long-term fertility. Techniques such as 'Low External-Input Sustainable Agriculture' (LEISA), which aim to develop agricultural systems that preserve long-term soil fertility and are affordable

KAREN TWINING/OXFAM

Evelynne Nyiramurehe lost all her crops in a landslide caused by floods

even by poor farmers, have barely begun to be tried in Rwanda. Although initial results are encouraging, the research establishments and ministry officials still favour the high-tech and high-input solutions that they have been trained to develop, rather than the low-tech, low-input approaches that would recognise the ability of the farmers to develop their own solutions.

The poverty trap

One of the central facts of a peasant farmer's life is that poverty of itself causes more poverty. The average cash income of a farming household in Rwanda has been calculated at just 26,183 RWF,[12] equivalent to about £187.00 per year. As plot sizes and soil fertility have declined, so poverty has increased and has become part of the problem of agricultural production.

In order to survive, farmers are forced to adopt short-term strategies, such as farming on the very steepest slopes, even though they know that such practices are not sustainable in the long term. As the fertility of the soil declines, so the farmer's crops struggle to thrive. If a plant disease spreads through the area, these struggling plants are affected far more seriously than those on the better soils of a wealthier neighbour, which can resist the disease to a greater extent.

Poverty also means that farmers have no capital to invest in such things as fertilisers, pesticides, or improved seeds, and they may not be able to risk trying a new technique that might help them to break out of the trap they are in. One report[13] suggests that only farmers with more than 1.5 hectares are able to invest in more economic production, while those with less land (about 69 per cent of farmers) have no choice but to adopt subsistence agriculture only. Faced with the responsibility of feeding the country, the government needs to encourage the production of market surpluses. The two-thirds of farmers who are seen as only growing for themselves, rather than for the market, are therefore considered a low priority for agricultural research or other forms of support. Instead the limited support that is available tends to go to those who are already slightly better off; these farmers are perceived not only to have more potential to increase production, but also to be more politically influential — and therefore it is more important to keep them happy.

Poverty also makes farmers vulnerable to merchants who buy their crops at rock-bottom prices when the family is most desperate (often just before harvest). To rub salt into the wound, the same merchant may then sell back the same crop to the farmer, at a far higher price, several months later when the harvest is over and food is scarce once more.

The government's response

Faced with this complex set of problems, the government has produced numerous policies designed to make Rwanda self-sufficient in food production. The major problem with these well-intentioned approaches is that they have been developed at the national level as country-wide panaceas. All too often they ignore the pressure on the individual farmer, trying to survive on his or her small plot. Two cases will illustrate the weaknesses of this strategy.

A policy of regional specialisation was designed to maximise national output by promoting those crops best suited to each area: for example, potatoes in the

Hills in Kivu Commune that were once covered in trees are now cultivated right up to their summits

VINCENT BANABAKINTU/OXFAM

mountains around Ruhengeri, cassava in Gitarama, and bananas in Kibungo. In reality this policy, although nominally still in place, has never been implemented, principally because what might be logical at the national level often does not make sense for individual farmers, basing their decisions on the household's needs for long-term food security, rather than on the national need for an overall increase in production. Not only, as we have seen, do decisions about the most appropriate crop to plant depend on factors specific to each family, but also the best decision for Rwanda may well not be the best for the individual household. Even though, for example, the yields of bananas grown at high altitudes are far less than those at low altitudes, the income that they provide for the farmer may still be far greater than for another crop, such as tea — even though the best-quality tea grows at high altitudes.

Too often, however, the logic of the peasant farmer is not understood by the 'experts' who work for ISAR, the government's national agricultural research institute. Perhaps because the proposals and funds for agricultural research usually come from Europe and the USA, there has been a tendency to try to develop seeds and animal varieties that are appropriate for intensified agro-industrial production. Unfortunately such solutions are often not suitable for the vast majority of Rwandan farmers (84 per cent of the total) who have less than two hectares of land and cannot therefore undertake agro-industrial production. One of ISAR's 12 research stations, for example, is dedicated to breeding a race of more productive cows. Unfortunately the animal produced is too big: it needs at least 1.2 hectares to support it. Thus by definition it is unusable by about 60 per cent of the population.

Useful results have been achieved in producing and distributing improved potato seeds; in inoculating soy and other beans with the bacteria they need to ensure efficient nitrogen-fixing; and in developing new varieties of many crops.

But ISAR has been noticeably unsuccessful in spreading even these innovations among the general farming population. Some of this is due to the sheer diversity of ecological zones and farming systems to be found in Rwanda that makes it difficult to match up a particular technology with a particular situation. More importantly agricultural administrators, researchers, and extension agents have failed to recognise, and put to use, the farmers' own detailed knowledge of their environment, and have ignored the peasant farmers' different priorities.

Christine, for example, a farmer in Butare, may sow a mix of seeds that is specific to the hill on which she lives, including up to 13 different varieties of bean, each with a slightly different profile of resistance to disease and climatic variation, so that — whatever happens — some of the varieties will produce something. While much work has been done to improve seed varieties, there has been a tendency to promote the single highest-yielding (but also highest-risk) variety, rather than improving the risk-reducing mix that farmers like Christine use. When the extension agent came from the commune, Christine and the other women farmers who met him were told that they should adopt the new seed: those who did not, implied the agent, would be regarded as ignorant and old-fashioned. Christine and her friends discussed the new seed and decided to use a little of it in a corner of their fields, but insisted on using their own mix, which they considered more reliable, for the rest of their plots.

The tendency of outside experts to presume that they have the technological answer to Rwanda's agricultural problems has been reinforced by the introduction of integrated rural development programmes in each region of the country, funded by international donors. (An integrated programme tries to tackle all aspects of development in a community, such as agriculture, health, education, and water supplies.) Despite a total investment in this sector alone of more than 60,000m

RWF (more than $600m) since Independence, the vast majority of this money has not gone into helping peasant farmers to grow enough food for their families. It has been spent on expensive infrastructure (cars, houses, offices, etc.) and salaries for the expatriate and local staff, and on the promotion of crops for export. There have also been a few cases of projects being used by those in charge to benefit their friends and political allies, but the real problem is not corruption. The real problem is that the pattern of spending has reinforced the dominance of the 'experts' over the local farmers, so that few of the resources provided have ever trickled down as far as the farmers who are supposed to benefit.

Is there a way out?

Underlying all these problems is the basic fact that peasant farmers as a class are powerless in Rwandan society. Until agricultural policy makers and extension agents learn to take the farmers' expertise seriously, inappropriate solutions will continue to be imposed on sceptical producers, who will abandon them as soon as they get the chance.

The way forward does not lie with any one technological or administrative reform, but with giving farmers the power to promote policies that are in their interests and reflect their priorities. Development 'experts' must learn to respect the farmers' expertise and draw lessons from it. Officials must devise economic and political structures that benefit local farmers, rather than the urban elite.

Such an approach will probably give a far higher priority to low-tech, low-input techniques which farmers, with their limited resources, can manage for themselves. Rwanda's farming problems are so diverse that there will probably be a place for many different solutions, which will ultimately be seen as complementary rather than competing.

Meanwhile, it is a sad commentary on the current political turmoil that the whole question of agricultural policy is almost ignored as the new political parties manoeuvre for power.

Development workers have much to learn from peasant farmers: Innocent Ntiruhongerwa (formerly Oxfam Project Officer) is seen here in conversation with Josepha Mujawabera, of the Kopabamu Co-operative

SU HOPKINS/OXFAM

An economy addicted to coffee

LIKE ALL OTHER COUNTRIES, Rwanda must export goods or services in order to earn the foreign currency to pay for imported commodities that it cannot produce for itself, and in order to pay off its debts. Almost 90 per cent of Rwanda's exports come from crops that are grown on just seven per cent of the country's agricultural land. So the temptation to increase the area used to cultivate export crops is intense.

Rwanda's most valuable export is coffee. The 'arabica' plant, producing mild, high-quality coffee beans, was first introduced into the country in the 1920s. Production expanded until by 1987 coffee exports, peaking at more than 42,000 tonnes, constituted 79 per cent of Rwanda's total export earnings. All the producers are smallholders, who are obliged to grow some coffee on their plots. During most of the 1980s the government assured them a guaranteed price of 125 RWF per kilo. The price was intended to remain stable, despite the variations in the world price. Until 1987 this meant that the price paid to producers was less than the strong world price — and the government earned huge sums from the coffee trade.

But the world price began to fall, and in 1989 Rwanda, like other small coffee-producing nations, was hit by the collapse of the International Coffee Agreement, which used to support prices to producing nations. The result of its collapse was that the price of coffee on the London market fell to half its 1980 level as the bigger exporters, such as Brazil, off-loaded their stocks. Smaller exporting nations, like Rwanda, have no influence over international prices. Since 1989 the world price has declined further, and after three years of heavily subsidising the price — and running up enormous debts to do so — the government was forced to reduce the price paid in Rwandan francs to the producer and to devalue the franc by 67 per cent. From the point of view of the World Bank, this restructuring of the price paid to producers was inevitable and welcome, as it brought producer prices into line with the realities of the world market. From the point of view of the peasant farmers it makes coffee production even less attractive than it was before.[14]

In 1989 there were 686,000 farmers, about 60 per cent of all smallholders, who grew an average of 150 coffee bushes each. They produced an average yield of 0.34 kg of saleable coffee from each bush, for which they received the guaranteed price of 125 RWF per kilo; this meant total earnings for an average farmer of 6,400 RWF.[15] In 1990 coffee production increased by 45 per cent on 1989 (which had been an exceptionally bad year). Production per tree averaged 0.49 kg. But the guaranteed price had been reduced to 115 RWF per kilo, so the income was 8,600 RWF. In November 1990 the Rwandan franc was devalued by 67 per cent, so that the farmer's purchasing power was even lower (see box).

Year	Prod'n (kg)	Guaranteed price/kg	RWF income	Exchange rate RWF/£	UK equiv. income (£)
1989	51.3	125	6,400	135	47.00
1990	74.2	115	8,500	225	38.00

The average farmer produced 45 per cent more — and earned about 20 per cent less.

While the government needs hard currency, the peasant farmer needs purchasing power irrespective of the currency used. Even before the price reduction, coffee bushes yielded a crop of substantially less value per hectare than, say, bananas or beans; now the differential is even worse, and many peasants are desperate to rip up their coffee plants in favour of other crops.

In the mean time, bad weather, declining soil fertility, and mistakes made in supplying pesticides have all combined to reduce the quality and quantity of production since 1987. These factors, combined with a fall in coffee prices that has only recently begun to be reversed and a production quota imposed on Rwanda by the International Coffee Organisation, mean that total government revenue has declined by almost 60 per cent.

'We can't eat tea'

Tea is Rwanda's second export crop, generating about 15 per cent of export receipts in 1988.[21] Unlike coffee, most tea

VINCENT BANABAKINTU/OXFAM

Projet Théicole: a tea plantation in Nshili-Kivu

is grown on estates. Between them, the tea plantations cover one per cent of Rwanda's cultivated area. In some areas, such as Nkuli, tea estates have been installed in areas that were previously densely settled by peasant farmers. Although some employment is provided on the tea plantations, the logic of many peasants is that tea cannot be eaten, and there are hungry people; therefore the plantations make no sense. Furthermore, land is an asset, and the right to use it can be passed on to the next generation and gives status to its owner. Money paid to the peasant in recompense for land expropriated for tea estates does not compensate for this fact. Once again there is a divergence between the logic of the central government and that of the individual farmer.

All except one of the tea estates in Rwanda are government-owned. All, except for the one in private hands, manage to lose money — despite producing some of the highest-quality tea in the world. So the World Bank is urging that much of the industry should be privatised, in order to increase its profitability.

Vanishing exports

Two other export crops that Rwanda has tried to develop are cinchona and pyrethrum. Cinchona is the raw material used in making quinine-based anti-malarial drugs. Growing as a tree, it is harvested every seven years, when the saplings are chopped down and the bark, which holds the raw material, is removed for processing. When the quinine market collapsed, the government refused to let peasant farmers up-root their trees, in the vain hope that the market would improve by the time they were ready to harvest. It has not, but most of the plantations are still there — except for the few which farmers have chopped down without permission.

The case of pyrethrum is similarly disappointing. As a newly independent country Rwanda already suffered from a shortage of hard currency. In collaboration

The rainforest habitat of animals like this baboon is under threat from large-scale development projects

with the European Development Fund it decided that it could grow pyrethrum for export. Pyrethrum is a natural weed killer, produced from a plant that looks rather like a large daisy. Half of the forests around the volcanoes in the north of Rwanda were cleared for pyrethrum plantations. The Batwa people who lived in the forest (along with traditional Batutsi pastoralists — the Bagogwe — and mountain gorillas, wild elephant, deer, and buffalo) were ignored by the project, which left them sitting in their clearings while their habitat, the forest, was felled around them. By the time the area was settled by landless farmers from other parts of the north, an artificial substitute for pyrethrum had been developed and the price had fallen. The parastatal company in charge of the project, OPYRWA, has never managed to make money, and the foreign exchange generated has been negligible. In the last few years there has been something of a revival of interest in pyrethrum, because its side-effects are less toxic than those of its artificial substitute. Perhaps after 25 years this project will eventually start generating real profits for Rwanda.

Tourism: from boom to bust

The major effect of the pyrethrum project was to push the Batwa, the gorillas, and the other wildlife in the forests around the volcanoes into competing with each other to survive, in an environment that was now only half its previous size. It was then that the North American naturalist, Dian Fossey, arrived in Rwanda with a mission to ensure the survival of the mountain gorillas. (It was a campaign for which she paid with her life. The story of her work with the gorillas and her subsequent murder is told in the film *Gorillas in the Mist*.) Against Fossey's wishes, the gorillas were turned into a tourist attraction. So successful was this initiative that by 1989 tourism was Rwanda's third largest earner of foreign exchange and, although the gorillas' future was still not guaranteed, their numbers were at least no longer declining.

Since 1990, however, incursions by the Rwandan Patriotic Front from Uganda have virtually closed off both of the country's national parks, and earnings from tourism are now almost zero. As and when the war ends, tourism could once again be developed — although there will be pressure to use the Akagera National

Park in the east for re-settling refugees returning from neighbouring countries, if an agreement can be reached for their repatriation. As with so many of the country's exports, there is a conflict of interest between the needs of the people for land to cultivate and the needs of the government to earn hard currency by exploiting the same land.

Tin prices melt away

Rwanda has remarkably few minerals or other natural resources that can be developed to yield hard-currency earnings. It does have small deposits of tin, however, which from 1930 onwards were mined in a crude way and provided almost 10 per cent of Rwanda's exports, as well as extra employment to about 25,000 men. In 1980, on the basis of a strong world price, SOMIRWA, the tin-mining company that was 51 per cent privately owned and 49 per cent government-owned, decided to invest in a large tin-refining plant. But the high price of tin had encouraged over-production around the world; and no sooner had SOMIRWA built its tin refinery than in October 1985 the International Tin Agreement collapsed. The price of tin on the world market fell by half. In 1986 SOMIRWA was declared bankrupt and tin exports ceased almost completely. In 1989 the industry was relaunched, with a loan from the World Bank; but with stagnant demand for tin, and continuing low prices, the outlook for the industry is not encouraging. Despite 17 years of inflation, the US dollar price of tin in 1993 is roughly the same as it was in 1976.

Export-led growth?

In order to pay for essential imports, Rwanda is chronically dependent on the export of primary products, mainly coffee and tea, to generate 95 per cent of its foreign exchange. As we have seen, that dependence makes it vulnerable to the swings of the commodities markets. Although Rwanda could earn more from these crops if their quality was improved and the government agencies that support farmers were managed more efficiently, it will not be easy as long as peasant farmers resist the government's directives that oblige them to cultivate such crops.

If, on the other hand, production could be increased, would export crops then provide a sound basis for economic growth in Rwanda? The commodities markets tend to move through cyclical patterns of boom and bust: short periods of high prices encourage increased production which, in turn, leads to longer periods of lower prices. How can this be reconciled with the constant needs of the country? And how will the emerging political structures divide the wealth earned from exports in times of prosperity, and share the burdens in times of slump?

A peasant farmer harvests coffee from his roadside plot. In 1990 the average farmer produced 45 per cent more coffee than in the previous year — and earned 20 per cent less.

Export or die ... or export and die?

IN A COUNTRY with a population of just 7.15 million people, of whom barely 300,000 operate in the monetary sector (as opposed to the subsistence sector) of the economy, Rwanda's internal market is too small to support many industries. As a result, the people and industries that constitute the country's tax base are few in number, and it is difficult for the government to raise enough taxes to cover its costs and for industry to work at a high enough capacity to be able to sell at internationally competitive prices. So what does the Rwandan economy consist of?

The rural market

A very high proportion — 93 per cent — of the Rwandan labour force is involved in agriculture, but the cash return they earn is so poor that the entire rural market is weak. Just how weak is shown by the way in which spending in rural areas varies with the seasons. The amount of money spent on health, for example, ought to vary according to how often people are ill. In fact, it varies according to the season, not because the illnesses vary, but because the amount of money declines during the hungry months, known as the *soudure*, of each year. In a bad year such as 1989, the decline in spending lasts the whole year, rather than just a few months.

Kigali: a boom town funded by peasant farmers

Most economic activity occurs in just one place: the capital, Kigali. Despite the problems 'on the hills', Kigali remains a boom town and is doubling in size every seven years. The population of the city has different tastes and needs from those of the rural population: the shops are full of imported foods and equipment. The urban elite travels by taxi or by car, which have to be imported, as does the fuel to run them. The roads they run on need bitumen that Rwanda does not have. The spare parts need to be imported. The steel for the buildings and their equipment all needs to be imported, as does a good proportion of the raw materials that go into the manufacture of beer by a subsidiary of Heineken.

How is this boom funded? The biggest employer in the country is the government, which employs about 7,000 people in the central administration, about 43,000 in the communes, and about 35,000 in the army. The salaries of the 7,000 in the central administration represent 45 per cent of the operating budget of the central government.[17] To pay the salaries of this workforce, the government must raise taxes. Until 1987 revenue was raised from taxes on imports and exports, and from making a profit on sales of coffee bought from the farmers at a fixed price and sold on the international market at a higher price. Thus although farmers produced 90

Kigali: a boom town that doubles in size every seven years

per cent of Rwanda's exports, much of the profit came back not to them but to the central government, whose spending was concentrated in Kigali. Since 1988 the government has had to borrow money to maintain its fixed prices to producers and its central expenditure. Kigali continued to boom, despite the fact that it was financed on borrowed funds.

A second source of Kigali's boom has been aid money from overseas, averaging more than US$200 million per year. As much as 80 per cent of this aid is spent on salaries and infrastructure, which (although necessary for the operation of the projects) tends to return to the economy of Kigali, while the trickle-down effect into the rural economy has been significantly less.

To try to reduce the concentration of economic activity in Kigali the government has abolished the export tax and replaced it with a flat-rate sales tax of 10 per cent, so transferring the impact of the tax from the rural producers alone to all those who are involved in the monetary economy.

The pressure for exports

Because of the recent decline in coffee prices, the collapse of tourism as a result of the war, and before that the collapse of the tin and cinchona industries, Rwanda's balance of payments has rapidly worsened since 1985 (despite windfall gains in 1986, caused by the temporary suspension of international coffee quotas), so that in 1989 the value of imported goods was 3.5 times greater than the total value of goods exported.[18] In the same year, half of the income from exports was spent on the single item of fuel. Given the need for all the steel, textiles, medicines, and so on that keep society functioning, it is not surprising that there is a tremendous pressure to increase exports.

But the terms of trade, or purchasing power, of Rwanda's exports, principally coffee, declined by 47 per cent between 1980 and 1988[19] (and have continued to fall rapidly since then). This meant that production would have had to increase by 89 per cent, merely to support the same level of imports. No other country has experienced a more drastic decline in its terms of trade over the same period.

The civil war caused the collapse of the once-lucrative tourist trade

The bitter medicine of structural adjustment

Not many options were open to the Rwandan government. Until 1990 it had set its face against adopting a Structural Adjustment Programme (SAP) at the behest of the International Monetary Fund, believing instead that by tightening its belt to deal with declining revenues it could hold out until an increase in coffee prices came to its rescue. In November 1990, with coffee prices continuing to fall and the bilateral donors making their further support conditional on Rwanda's signing an agreement with the IMF and World Bank, the Rwandan government finally brought its five years of resistance to an end and accepted the inevitable: a Structural Adjustment Programme under IMF 'tutelage'.

This package involved a 67 per cent devaluation of the Rwandan franc, a freeze in salaries, plans for privatising many of the parastatal businesses, plans to reduce the administrative hurdles that discouraged business initiatives, and a reduction of export tariffs in order to encourage international trade. In addition, each sector of the Rwandan economy was to be examined to see how it could be made more productive. The SAP provided new loans over a number of years, in the expectation that the balance of payments would eventually improve, as businesses responded to the reforms.

The logic behind these reforms was that the Rwandan franc was overvalued, so making the country's exports too expensive to be competitive on the world market. The devaluation (followed by another, by 15 per cent, in 1992) was supposed to increase the profitability of exports, and encourage production. As the quantity of coffee produced and the dollar price that it earns are largely determined by the international market (which is dominated by Brazil), Rwanda will receive the same dollar price for its exports as it did before the devaluations. The effect of the devaluations is that the number of Rwandan francs earned for that same quantity of dollars has increased. Unfortunately this does not mean that everyone is richer, because the imported goods which the recipient of those Rwandan francs wants to buy have increased in price correspondingly.

The price the government had to pay for the introduction of the SAP was a reduction in its own spending: the size of the civil service was cut, and businesses that had previously been in government hands were privatised. All this took place a few weeks after the start of the war, with all the constraints which that introduced, and at the same time as further falls in coffee prices. So it was inevitable that exports did not achieve their targeted growth rate, but declined instead, with coffee production falling back by 22 per cent in 1991.[20]

In the short term, what this policy means is that all the people who earn their income in Rwandan francs face increased prices for imported goods, while the income of government agencies and businesses is strengthened. The mass of the population whose incomes are fixed and paid in Rwandan francs immediately had to pay 67 per cent more for medicines, for example, and one study showed that prices for a range of basic necessities in Kigali had, on average, increased by about 50 per cent during the first seven months of the programme.[21] (The architects of the Structural Adjustment Programme had forecast inflation of just 28 per cent for the first year.) So people will tend to have less purchasing power for health care, education, and other necessities — at the same time as the Structural Adjustment Programme requires them to pay a larger proportion of costs in these sectors. (This will happen despite the fact that by means of their newly acquired veto of the national budget, the multilateral funding agencies are insisting that the proportion of the budget spent on these sectors should increase.)

The government and its donors hope that in the long run the policies of liberalising trade will create greater wealth for Rwanda by putting its

One effect of economic structural adjustment is to open Rwanda's market to imported goods from the industrialised North

ADRIAN ARBIB/OXFAM

THE POWER
OF LOVE

GUINNESS
THE POWER

economy on a sounder footing. In the short term, however, most people have to swallow the bitter medicine of declining purchasing power when they are already on or below the poverty line.

The trade trap

It seems that all the odds are stacked against the Rwandan economy: its dependence on Northern imports, the country's location 1,500 km from the nearest ports (which means crippling transport costs for its exports), its limited natural resources, and its growing population are all important factors in the country's chronic and worsening poverty. By 1990 there was no disputing that the Rwandan economy was out of balance and that changes had to be introduced. But the economic crisis that led to the Structural Adjustment Programme in Rwanda is not an isolated phenomenon: it has been happening throughout Africa.

In the years between 1980 and 1986, the value of primary products exported from Africa fell by half, driven down by deteriorating terms of trade.[22] Governments throughout Africa have been obliged to reduce the incomes of their entire populations, to restore economic viability to the structures of central government.

In the case of Rwanda, although there have been mistakes in government policies, in particular in the management

of the coffee price equalisation fund, the economy has on the whole been well managed. The money was stable and levels of inflation, foreign debt, and corruption were all low. It is not easy to say (as has been said of some other countries): 'It's all their own fault'. Once the price of coffee collapsed after 1989, it was inevitable that the Rwandan government would have to adjust to the drop in national earnings by cutting the value of people's incomes. It can be argued that they would have saved themselves a lot of trouble if they had done this earlier; but it could also be argued that it is not fair for Rwandan farmers to pay to keep down the cost of the Northern consumer's tea and coffee.

A key element of the Structural Adjustment Programme is to encourage more exports. But the same policy is being promoted to poor countries all around the world, and they find themselves caught in a trade trap: the more they produce, the lower the price falls on the world market. In theory, the country with the greatest comparative advantage should win the competition, but the real winner seems likely to be the North, which will continue to procure its raw materials at low prices — while exporting countries in the South, divided and competing among themselves, over-produce and force prices ever lower in a vain search for foreign currency. If they try to add value to their raw commodities by processing them, they run into tariff barriers imposed by the rich industrialised nations, which protect the market share of large multi-national companies. Raw coffee beans entering the European Community, for instance, encounter a tariff of 9 per cent; but roasted ground coffee is penalised by a tariff of 16.5 per cent, and instant coffee carries a tariff of 18 per cent. In Japan the tariff on instant coffee is 20.5 per cent.

Rwandans are asking how often the poor of the South will have to 'structurally adjust' to ever greater poverty, while the countries of the already rich North get together to fix the rules of that trade to their own advantage.

Alternative paths to development

RWANDA, as we have seen, is over-dependent on a few export crops. And it has thousands of young people entering the workforce every year, seeking employment. Is there a way in which the Rwandan economy can be restructured to solve these two problems?

Urban industries?

Some suggest that Rwanda should follow the model of Taiwan or Singapore, by seeking to develop an industrial sector to make use of the country's greatest resource: its population. But only six per cent of the population have completed secondary school, and fewer than one per cent have been to university. In an industrial environment in which technological excellence is a key component of success, Rwanda's workforce is under-qualified, inexperienced, and not particularly cheap by world standards. The shortage of foreign exchange for the purchase of imported materials is a further obstacle to industrialisation.

Rural industries?

As an alternative to intensive industrialisation, it might be possible to develop rural industries that are complementary to Rwanda's basic activity of agricultural production. This could involve small-scale industries, providing basic equipment to farmers (such as hoes, axes, stoves, and furniture) or processing their produce through drying, milling, and packaging. There have been some

efforts in this direction, but progress has been slow because of the poor level of technical training provided by the Centres for Integrated Rural and Technical Training, the CERAIs, and the limited purchasing power in rural areas that makes it difficult to generate a local market in the processed items.

Bee-keeping in Nyagasambu: Pauline Mukamana and Agnes Mujaweyezu working on a hive owned by their co-operative

VINCENT BANABAKINTU/OXFAM

Handicrafts?

So far, the most visible forms of non-agricultural employment are found in the production of handicrafts such as baskets, mats, embroidery, and knitting. In many cases there is a tendency to produce simply for the sake of it, without really seeking to meet the needs of a particular market. The income generated is often pitifully small, and the enterprises are unlikely either to generate sustainable long-term employment or to survive, once external support is withdrawn. But there are workshops, such as KIAKA in Gisenyi and those supplying COPIMAR, a co-operative marketing agent in Kigali, that have managed to create a sustainable rural industry, providing viable employment. The challenge for such enterprises is to find urban and even international markets for their products.

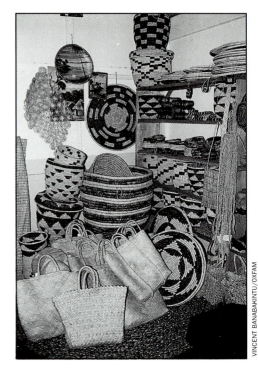

VINCENT BANABAKINTU/OXFAM

Public works?

One way of providing work in rural areas is to employ large numbers of labourers on public works (as has been proposed as part of the package of measures to alleviate the impact of the Structural Adjustment Programme). This strategy has already been used for the construction of some roads and could perhaps be extended to the creation of agricultural terraces, to combat the problem of soil erosion on steep slopes. Although such programmes are not sustainable in the long term, they do at least put cash into the rural economy, and should provide infrastructure which will bring lasting help to the communities concerned. The danger is that once an activity such as terracing is started on this basis, individuals will not undertake it for themselves without payment: in the end the process of change could be discouraged rather than promoted.

In reality there is no one path for Rwanda to pursue: to paraphrase Pope John Paul II when he visited Rwanda in 1990, the Land of a Thousand Hills often seems like the Land of a Thousand Problems, and to solve them it needs to become the Land of a Thousand Solutions.

The Atacomu Weaving Co-operative in Muhazi Commune uses sisal leaves and banana leaves to make mats and bags

VINCENT BANABAKINTU/OXFAM

Urbanisation: the bright lights beckon

RWANDA IS REMARKABLE for the fact that 93 per cent of its population live in the countryside, and only 7 per cent in towns. Not only are there few towns but, in most areas of the country, except in the extreme north around Lake Bulero, there are very few villages either. Traditionally people live on their own plots of land, scattered across the hills. Unlike in Tanzania and Burundi, there has not been a policy of creating villages and obliging people to settle in them. Urbanising factors such as government offices, market places, health centres, schools, and churches have often been located away from each other so that concentrations of people in villages or towns have not developed naturally.

The effect of this has been to discourage non-agricultural economic activity, except in the regional and national centres, which are all growing rapidly. While the regional centres remain small, the capital, Kigali, now has a population of around 233,000[23] and is supposedly doubling in size every seven years. Kigali, created by the Germans in 1908, had a population of just 8,000 at the time of Independence in 1962. Much of its growth has been due to the concentration of wealth generated by export crops and the international aid missions within the capital. It has been estimated that Kigali alone accounts for 50 per cent of the circulation of money within Rwanda. It is hardly surprising that (despite frequent attempts by the government to restrict migration from the rural areas into the capital city) it continues to grow at the rate of 10 per cent every year.

In effect, the rapid growth of Kigali is probably the only way to absorb significant numbers of those who can no longer be supported by agriculture. The migrants manage to survive by activities like itinerant selling, shoe shining, and porterage, but this kind of small-scale enterprise is discouraged by restrictive official policies. As the possibilities of migration from Rwanda become more limited, urbanisation must be recognised as an option to be managed, rather than prevented.

The story of Gapiri and his gang

Urbanisation will never be painless, as the cases of Gapiri, Ignace, Thomas, and Richard suggest. They are four of the many hundreds of young boys who live on the streets of Kigali and rush to guard your car whenever you stop to go shopping. Their patch is in the centre of town. If another boy comes along and wants to work in their area, they beat him up; but if he puts up with this treatment for about five days, they will let him into their gang.

On average they earn at least 100 RWF (about 40 pence) each working day, which is enough to get something to eat. The main problem is Sundays and holidays, when there is no custom: if they have not put money aside, they have to go hungry on these days. When the political parties hold their demonstrations, the leaders of each gang are paid a few hundred francs to join in. Gapiri and his gang enjoy these events, partly because they are also given food.

Before the war there were more people on the streets, but then those without the proper papers, including Gapiri, were sent home to their own communes. His home was in Gitarama, which he left at the age of 15 in 1988. After a month he had returned to Kigali and taken up his old work.

What do they think of multi-party politics? In view of their marginalisation in society it is perhaps surprising that they have detected a change. They say that —

Street kids at the Club Rafiki (the Friendship Club), Kigali

apart from the military captain who tries to beat them up whenever he sees them wearing the colours of an opposition party — in general they are treated rather better now than before. It used to be that if the police caught you they would beat you, and if you didn't pay a £2.00 fine (which went straight into the pockets of the police) they would put you in prison. There you could starve, if you didn't have any family to bring you food. But now the authorities are not so hostile, and the new government may bring in less restrictive laws that would allow street traders to operate openly.

For the future, their ambitions are varied. Gapiri and Ignace would like some training, but it has to be interesting — Ignace has tried it and kept falling asleep until they kicked him out — and it should provide a meal, so they would not have to work on the streets to earn money for food. Thomas, who is just 13 years old, seemed when he was interviewed for this book to see his life on the street as an idyllic existence, and aspired to nothing more than a *carton*: a tray full of sweets and cigarettes, from which he could sell to the public. Such a tray, fully stocked, would cost about £15.00. Gapiri interjected to say

that he had once been given a tray by a generous man working at Bralirwa (the brewery), but he did not have the necessary 'protection' from anyone in the police or army, and his stock was soon stolen.

Without a tray or some other improved source of income, they could not hope to earn enough money to be able to marry. Instead they would have to carry on visiting various *copines* (girlfriends) who would sleep with them for a few hundred francs. And AIDS? Yes, they had heard of it and had seen friends die of it, but it was not high on their list of priority problems.

The Rwandan Scouts Association, the Friendship Club (Club Rafiki), and the churches are already working well with the poor of Kigali, including its street children and unemployed labourers. All the new political parties have numerous business people among their leaders; if they gain power in the future, will they be any more sympathetic to this informal sector than previous governments? Will they try to use migration to the cities as a constructive alternative to rural poverty, or will the cities just become a dumping ground to be tolerated until the poor begin to be a nuisance?

Migration: the never-ending search for land

MIGRATION has always been one of the survival strategies of poor people in the Great Lakes region. From the point of view of a poor family, it means fewer mouths to feed from their smallholding. From the point of view of the country as a whole, it can mean either that previously un-farmed lands are opened up or, if the migrant leaves the country, there is one less stomach to fill.

Internal migration

With the vast number of different agricultural zones produced by the varying altitudes, soils, and climates of Rwanda, there is usually someone not too far away whose crops are in need of labour and who is prepared to pay for it (if only with a small amount of food at the end of the day). For many years there have been seasonal movements of workers to projects such as tree-planting on the Nile-Zaire crest, or tea-picking in Burundi. This sort of migration is temporary and relatively local.

Since Independence, more organised migration within the country has been a part of official agricultural policy. People from areas of land shortage (Gisenyi, Ruhengeri, Butare, and Gikongoro in particular) have been settled in the area around the Volcanoes National Park, in certain other areas that were previously forested, in valley-bottom land[24] that used to be reserved for the use of cattle, and in large areas in the east, especially the Mutara and the Bugesera. Some of the land thus settled was very fertile, especially that around the Volcanoes National Park, where there are excellent volcanic soils, and the valley-bottom lands. But other areas, such as the Mutara, with poorer soils, lower rainfall, and endemic diseases, are only marginal. This policy of expansion within Rwanda cannot be continued for much longer: those spaces that are still temptingly empty, such as Nyungwe Forest in the south-west and the Akagera National Park in the east, would probably not be able to support agriculture on a sustainable basis.

Besides the officially organised settlement of new lands, people from areas of land shortage have unofficially resettled themselves in areas perceived as having land available. Thus many thousands of people (possibly around 164,000[25]) have moved to the Bugesera and by one means or another have sought to obtain land. But less and less is available, especially as Rwandans who had settled in Tanzania are sent back and are reclaiming the land they had abandoned.

The overall effect of this internal migration has been to open land up to intensive cultivation — land that was previously either unused or used less intensively for pasturing cattle or hunting and gathering. As each of these activities is associated with a particular ethnic group — extensive cattle herding

Fields of potatoes on deforested slopes, Kivu Province: evidence of the severe shortage of land in Rwanda

VINCENT BANABAKINTU/OXFAM

VINCENT BANABAKINTU/OXFAM

For landless people, there is often no option but to clear space in forest areas

(pastoralism) with the Batutsi, hunting and gathering with the forest Batwa, and cultivation with the Bahutu — the change in land use has been part and parcel of ethnic conflict in the country. If large numbers of Batutsi refugees do return one day to Rwanda, they will probably be unable to practise their customary forms of extensive land use, such as pastoralism, because the land is simply no longer available to support it.

Migration beyond Rwanda

As long ago as 1920 the Belgian colonial authorities set up an organisation to manage the resettlement of people from the most densely populated parts of Rwanda to unsettled parts of neighbouring Zaire. Over the years up until 1959 about 264,000[26] were resettled under this scheme. Even so, such formal schemes have been dwarfed in their impact by informal, independent migrations that individuals have undertaken in search of land, or work, or safety from political persecution in the surrounding countries of Uganda, Burundi, Zaire, and Tanzania.

This massive influx of Banyarwanda people to the neighbouring countries, as refugees and as economic migrants, has caused problems for the host nations. They are unpopular because they are seen as having gained land, political power, and economic success at the expense of the host community; like refugees anywhere, they are accused of failing to assimilate themselves into their country of refuge. So the Banyarwanda are often targeted as scapegoats during periods of economic decline and political turbulence. The attacks on them were particularly severe in Uganda in the early 1980s, which led to a sense among the refugees that they had nowhere that they could call home. In Tanzania, Zaire, and Burundi the pressures were less violent, but they were still present: at the same time as the Rwandan Patriotic Front's army was trying to return to Rwanda by force, the Tanzanian government insisted on a treaty with the Rwandan government under which all illegal immigrants from Rwanda since 1986 would be repatriated, and those who had arrived before 1986 would be given Tanzanian citizenship. As the 30,000 people forced to return came from the poorest parts of Rwanda with the least land available, the prospects of these returnees are gloomy indeed.[27]

Joseph's story

Joseph is a farmer from Nyakizu in Butare. Three years ago he and his wife acknowledged that the family plot in Nyakizu was never going to be able to support them and their three children. They had been aware of it for a while, but the crop failure in 1989 brought home the urgency of the situation and forced them to decide what to do.

Even before the poor crop had been harvested, Joseph walked to the Bugesera, about 120 km away, to see if there was any land available. He found that most of the land was already taken, that many others were looking, and that the communal authorities were hostile to new people coming in. But eventually he found a farmer who was prepared to lease him some land, because he had only one son and wanted some extra cash to pay for his marriage. Joseph then went back to Nyakizu to fetch the rest of the family.

On arriving back in Nyakizu he found the situation even worse than he had expected: the harvest had been very bad, there had been thefts from the fields, and many others were trying to leave to find land elsewhere. Some men had simply gone off and left their wives and children behind, others had sold everything, including their land and their houses (which were being broken down for their wood and roofing tiles).

Joseph could not sell his straw-covered house, because it had no roofing tiles or corrugated iron sheets that had a market value. His parents and brother needed his land to survive, so he could not sell that either. Instead he and his wife sold their coffee crop, while it was still unharvested, to a merchant who gave them a very low price for it, and left for Bugesera.

The journey was difficult: the youngest child became sick, but they could not take her to a health centre because they needed what money they had to set themselves up in Bugesera. They slept in the open for three nights, in unseasonal rain which made things very cold and uncomfortable.

When they arrived in Bugesera, they were intercepted by an official from the commune who checked their papers and told them they could not stay. It took a whole day to sort the problem out. When they found the farmer who had promised them the land, he asked for more money than originally agreed. They had no more money, so they had to go elsewhere. After a week of searching, which was much more difficult with the whole family in tow, they finally found a small plot at Nyamata which the owner would allow them to use for the next season — but without any guarantee for the future.

A typical straw-roofed house, with banana trees in the background

The plot was not very good, but they planted beans and sorghum in October and hoped for the best. Because their position was not recognised by the commune, they could not have sent their children to school even if they had had the money to do so. The period up until December, when they could start eating some of the beans, was very difficult, and they survived only with the help of the land owner, who occasionally gave them some food in return for a day's work.

Joseph went to Tanzania early in the year to look for land. Just as he arrived, the authorities decided that there were too many Rwandans illegally settled in that area of north-western Tanzania; everyone who had arrived since 1986 would be sent back to Rwanda. Many of the people there had come, like Joseph, from the area around Nyakizu, with a brief stay in the Bugesera first. Joseph hurried back to Nyamata to try to find a better plot of land and make more permanent arrangements before these people started to come back.

In the end he went back to the first farmer and renewed their arrangement. Although it was still not recognised by the authorities (so that if the farmer died, his son might not honour his father's agreement), it was better than their current situation and therefore worth trying.

When, in March 1990, the first people started arriving back from Tanzania, there was a great deal of confusion. Some had lent their houses and land to others and wanted them back; others had sold them without their families' permission — which was illegal and therefore put everyone in a difficult situation. Still others had simply abandoned their families when they had left the Bugesera, and had taken new wives in Tanzania. Theirs was not exactly a joyous homecoming. For many there was nothing to come back to, and some of them either went to the local parish in search of charity or simply turned straight around and headed back to Tanzania.

Joseph and his family live from day to day, concentrating on short-term survival, and trying not to think what the future might hold.

What of the future?

The problems posed by the increasing limits on migration are shown by research done for the National Enquiry into Household Expenditure in 1984. Somewhat to the researchers' surprise, they found that poverty — as measured in this case by food consumption per capita — was not most severe among the 20 per cent with the least land, but rather among the next 20 per cent with rather more land.[28] The suggested reason for this was that those with the least land had been forced to adopt the strategy of migration for some members of the family in order for the other members to survive. Once some had left, there was more food for those remaining. Meanwhile those with a bit more land struggled on, trying to make ends meet, and suffered progressively as the years went by. If migration in search of land is not an option in the future, what strategies will later generations adopt in order to survive?

The environment: a country living off its capital

> *Ukandagira isi ntayibabaza.* — He who walks upon the earth doesn't make it suffer. (Rwandan proverb)

THE LUSH GREEN LAND of Rwanda that is glimpsed in tourist brochures and television wildlife documentaries is not the whole picture. Rwanda's natural environment is fragile, and increasingly threatened by poverty.

Warning signs in the woodlands ...

About 9 per cent of Rwanda's surface is covered by forest. Almost two-thirds of the woodland is natural; it is recognised as important to the local climate and wildlife, and therefore in need of protection. The forests of Nyungwe and the Virunga National Park, home to the last surviving mountain gorillas, are environmental reserves of international importance.

But people need wood for cooking and heating water. With no other fuel to hand, women are having to walk for hours each day to find wood; each year they travel farther and farther, on tiring journeys over the hills, to find less and less.

In 1986 the Forestry Department estimated that each year Rwanda as a whole was using 2.3 million cubic metres of wood more than it was producing. To reduce this deficit would require a 100 per cent increase in wood production. Even though the figures were tentative, the government has pushed ahead with its programme of planting trees in wood lots, knowing that the rapidly increasing population is adding to the demand for wood every year.

Through the use of *umuganda*

(community labour) the area of wood lots had already been doubled between 1980 and 1986, and that growth has continued since, with the aim of doubling the area of wood lots again before 2000 AD.

The main tree planted has been eucalyptus, which now forms 80 per cent of Rwanda's wood-lots. It has the advantages of growing very quickly, of growing up again when it has been coppiced, being able to grow on barren soils, and being suitable for both fuel and construction. On the other hand, agriculturalists hate it with a passion, because it leaves the soils barren of nutrients. This is inevitable, the foresters argue, because eucalyptus grows so quickly. Without eucalyptus, they say, the destruction of other forest areas would have been far worse during the past ten years.

It is true that eucalyptus has made an essential contribution to solving the country's wood deficit. But Rwanda is in the vulnerable position of being over-dependent on this one species of tree, and in the future it must diversify to other species — preferably ones that can be combined with food production and animal husbandry.

The government's Forestry Plan estimates that 91 per cent of Rwanda's timber is used for domestic fuel, mainly for cooking. It set itself the objective of improving the efficiency of stoves by 1.5 per cent each year, but so far little progress has been made. In areas that are particularly short of wood, women are using small twigs (which means they have to watch the fire more closely) and are cooking less frequently, sometimes going for several days without cooked food; but the stoves they are using have not yet changed.

43

VINCENT BANABAKINTU/OXFAM

Wood has a wide variety of uses in Rwanda, as shown by this home-made wooden scooter, used for transporting sugar cane

... and good news on the water front

Women also have to fetch water for their families. Here, remarkably, things have improved over the years. By 1990, 70 per cent of Rwandan families had access to piped water that was generally of good quality. Most of these systems use gravity to bring water down from springs to public stand-points, where people can collect it in jerry cans. Hours of women's time is thus saved, and water-borne diseases avoided, thanks to *umuganda* — the system of community labour which constructed the water supplies. Local non-governmental organisations are continuing to put in gravity systems throughout the country, to spread the benefits of safe water, and to keep up with the demand created by the rising population.

Profit and loss in the environment

Since the start of the war, nearly one million people have been displaced from their homes in the north to live in temporary shelters and survive as best they can farther south. This has done huge damage to carefully conserved forest resources. Despite the pressure of shortages of land, Rwanda has until recently succeeded in avoiding an environmental disaster, and has made tremendous efforts to stay ahead of the problems that often accompany the expansion of agricultural production. This expansion has mostly occurred through extending cultivation into woodlands, pastures, and scrub — at the expense of the hunter-gatherers and pastoralists who previously used these areas. The possibilities of further extension are increasingly limited to environmental reserves such as the Nyungwe Forest, the Nyabirongo Valley, and the Akagera National Park. The demand for land for both cultivators and pastoralists, and the association of each activity with different ethnic groups, means that the management of the environment is as fundamentally political as any other area of life in Rwanda.

A third strategy is to increase the production of wood on the individual smallholders' farms. Although useful work has been done to discover which types of trees are the most suitable and combine best with the crops growing beneath them, most farmers feel that the trees are taking up space that they can ill afford to lose. Planting trees on land is a traditional sign of ownership of that land. Because women cannot own land, they cannot plant trees. Because men do not have to spend hours fetching wood, they are less motivated to resolve the problem than women would be. Until the problem of fuel-wood supply becomes a higher priority for men, the solutions proposed will continue to be top-down campaigns of compulsory tree planting, rather than the full integration of wood production into smallholders' farming systems.

At present and for the foreseeable future, the figures for supply and demand just do not add up — despite the remarkable work that has been done in planting new trees over the past ten years. And much of that progress has now been undone by the civil war and violent unrest, as a result of which thousands of hectares of forest have been burnt down. Thousands of women all over the country will have to carry on walking farther to get what they need.

Hunters and gatherers in a disappearing world

THE FATE OF THE FOREST is inextricably linked to the fate of the most vulnerable of all Rwanda's people: the Batwa, whose future seems to have been decided without their ever being consulted. The Batwa (who actually consist of two groups: those who make a living from pottery, and those who live by hunting and gathering in the forest) form less than one per cent of the population; the forest Batwa, known as the Impunyu, living almost solely in Ruhengeri and Gisenyi, number fewer than 5,000 men, women, and children. They are often mistrusted by their fellow Rwandans, who consider them to be barely civilised.

Nahimana's story

Nahimana, an Impunyu man aged about 40, lives in Gisenyi. When his mother was young, in the 1930s, the Impunyu used to hunt buffalo, elephant, wild boar, and antelopes. She told him that at that time the forest stretched without a break from Gishwati up to the volcanoes and on into Zaire. There was game in abundance, and the Impunyu roamed widely through the rainforest.

Soon after Independence in the 1960s the European Community funded a major project to produce pyrethrum (an insecticide made from plants) on the slopes of the volcanoes. Large tracts of forest were cleared, and this broke the link between the forest and the wildlife reserves of Zaire. The planners ignored the very existence of the Impunyu, who were left in their clearings as the forest around them was cut down and the land allocated to cultivators. The Gishwati Forest became even more isolated from the forests of Zaire when a road was cut

from Ruhengeri to Gisenyi and a military camp was built at Bigogwe. As a result, large game soon disappeared from the Rwandan forest. The few remaining animals were hunted out, and wood was cut for fuel. To save the forest, the government banned the Impunyu from living there.

Things got worse and worse for the Batwa. In the late 1970s many in Gisenyi suffered from famine. By 1980 the quality of their forest environment was still more diminished and another project aimed at saving the Gishwati Forest was agreed, this time with World Bank funding. Once again the existence of the Impunyu was ignored: 25,000 hectares of the remaining 30,000 hectares of forest were cut down

VINCENT BANABAKINTU/OXFAM

Deprived of their traditional hunting grounds, Batwa communities face an uncertain future

'There is no other future than the hoe': many Batwa, like these women, have been obliged to take up cultivation in order to survive

and converted to pasture, which was almost all allocated to friends and relations of the President. Between 1980 and 1986 Nahimana and his family tried to settle 13 different plots of land, only to have them taken away and given to a well-placed family for use as a cattle ranch. The Impunyu managed to survive by clearing the forest and making charcoal for sale to the surrounding population.

In 1987 the President officially recognised the plight of the Impunyu. Since then the authorities have been trying to find land for them, and encouraging the Impunyu to come to terms with the inevitable: to become cultivators like everyone else.

This programme has brought some benefits to Nahimana: his children are doing well in school and he is successfully cultivating. On the surface he has left his traditional culture behind. Asked about the future, he says that — except for those with education — 'there is no other future than the hoe': there is no going back to the forest. Asked for his views on the new political parties, he offers a simple but broadly accurate analysis: 'There are only two parties that count: the MRND and the MDR — and they're both Hutu.' Their new life-style as cultivators is irreversible, but Nahimana, and the other Impunyu like him, still remember who they are and what they have had taken from them.

Can Batwa communities survive with their traditional cultures intact?

Population: from 2 to 10 million in 60 years

THE POPULATION of Rwanda is growing at a rate of 3.1 per cent each year[29] — one of the highest growth rates in the world. On average, every woman will give birth to at least six live children. Half the population is under the age of 15, so the rate of increase is bound to grow further, as young women reach child-bearing age. From two million inhabitants in 1940, the population in 1991 was estimated to have reached 7.15 million. If it increases at the rate of 3.1 per cent each year, the population of Rwanda will reach 10 million by 2002 AD.

It has become a cliché in development circles to assert that, from the peasant farmers' point of view, having a large number of children makes economic sense: they provide labour, people to look after you in your old age, social status in the community, and sons to inherit your land ·so that it stays in the family. But there are disadvantages as well as benefits.

> *Urukwavu rukuze rwonka abana.* — An old hare sucks at the teat of its young. (When the parents grow old, it's the children's turn to look after them.) (Rwandan proverb)

The story of Marie-Rose Kabageni

Marie-Rose Kabageni is a smiling, bright-eyed woman of 55, living in Muganza commune in the south of Rwanda. She has eight children between the ages of 36 and 13 years. Six are girls; one is married and lives in a neighbouring commune, and a second is about to get married. Two are boys; one serves in the Rwandan army, and the other has migrated, probably to Tanzania, and has lost contact with his mother. All the children were educated to the end of primary school.

After the birth of Marie-Rose's eighth child in 1978, her husband abandoned her

KAREN TWINING/OXFAM

Shepherd boys in Kivu Commune: children are a gift from God, a source of status, and a supply of labour

and went to work in Uganda. He has never been back or contacted her since then. She has managed alone to support the family from the small plot around her house, and from land that she is allowed to use in the valley bottom about 300 metres away.

Marie-Rose hopes for support from her soldier son in her old age. Her daughters will move away as they marry, but if they don't go too far, she hopes they will also help her in her old age.

The story of Johanni and Teodosia

In contrast to the story of Marie-Rose, the case of her neighbours, Johanni-Eudes Gatabazi and his wife Teodosia Muhandori, both 38 years old, suggests that attitudes are slowly changing.

Married with five children between the ages of 18 and 1 year, Teodosia and Johanni have a small plot of land on the side of the valley. They used to grow beans in between the banana trees, but the yields were not good, so they have changed to growing sweet potatoes. With the help of land farmed in the valley bottom, the family gets by and is able to buy clothes, beans, school equipment, paraffin, salt, and soap.

Asked about the future, Johanni says that he would prefer not to have any more children, because that would mean more mouths to feed and more people to share the inheritance of the tiny plot of family land. Johanni says that he and Teodosia are considering using some form of family planning. 'Things have changed,' he says, 'because now there are local people who promote the use of family planning. Even the Catholic Church is in favour of family planning using natural methods.'

The economic logic of family planning is slowly changing, but even when it does, it takes a long time to influence people's decisions. When asked whether he is actually going to seek some form of contraception, Johanni is unsure, and says simply that he will think about it when the youngest child is weaned.

Social attitudes to family planning

Rwandan culture has always placed great value on children. They are regarded as a gift from God, and a source of status both for the woman who gives birth to them and for their father. But in recent times it has become a source of social shame if a father cannot pay for his children's education, and cannot provide them with an inheritance. As the sizes of family plots decline and the cost of education increases, so people are becoming aware of the disadvantages, as well as the benefits, of having a large family.

The problem for women is that even if they do want to use contraception, either to delay or to prevent a pregnancy, often it is their husbands who take the final decision. Surveys show that many more women would like to use family-planning methods than actually do. This suggests that campaigns to promote contraception should focus on men, because — as things are — they are the ones who can translate women's wishes into action.

The role of the Catholic Church

A second constraint on the implementation of family planning in Rwanda has been the strength of the Catholic Church, the inflexibility of its views on family planning, and the fact that it runs one-third of the country's health centres. Even though in 1987 the Catholic bishops recognised that the problem of population growth was serious,[30] the Church did not modify its official line: that only natural family planning was acceptable. Many lay Catholics in Rwanda argued[31] for a change of policy, but it was not until the visit of the Pope in 1990 that any significant change occurred. It was not what he said, but what he didn't say, that was significant. Since the visit, most Rwandan bishops, following his example, have maintained silence on the subject. Though personally opposed to any form of 'artificial' contraception, they have tacitly agreed to allow the staff who run their health centres to use their discretion

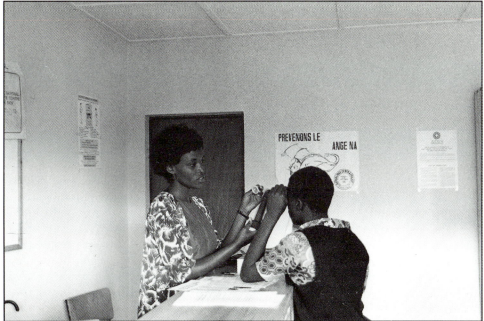

How to use a
condom: the rate
of contraceptive
use has increased
rapidly in Rwanda
in recent years

in deciding whether to offer family-planning services. This means that whereas before the Pope's visit none of the Catholic health centres provided the full range of family-planning services, just 18 months later half of them were doing so, and there are hopes that the rest will follow suit soon.

The government's response

In 1981 the National Office of Population Activities (ONAPO) was created, aiming to balance population growth with national resources. When the first phase of funding from USAID (the United States Agency for International Development) came to an end in 1988, the results of ONAPO's work were not encouraging: just 4 per cent of women were recorded as using any form of contraception.

Since then the rates of contraceptive use have increased rapidly, for several reasons. Firstly there was a severe food shortage in the south-west of the country in 1989, which brought home to everyone just how precarious the national food supplies were. Secondly, the government adopted a National Population Policy in June 1990, which gave the whole programme a higher priority than before. Thirdly, a start was

made on integrating the family-planning services into the hospitals and health centres run by the Ministry of Health.

Combined with the change in the attitude of the Catholic Church, the effect of all these convergent forces was that the rate of contraceptive use had risen to 9.6 per cent in 1990 and to between 12 per cent and 13.6 per cent in 1991. Despite this progress, there remain many problems to overcome before the programme will have a noticeable impact on the country's population growth rate. If the programme achieved a 35 per cent rate of contraceptive usage by the year 2000, the population would still increase to almost 10 million during the same period. The main impact would be on individual women, whose child-bearing burden would be considerably lightened.

The whole question of reproduction is an intensely personal matter. Many Rwandans resent what they see as external pressure to limit the country's population, even if they accept that the rate of population growth is a problem. So it is all the more significant that ONAPO's family-planning programme is beginning to have some impact at last.

49

Health for some by the year 2000

Umutindi ntapfa arahuhuka — A poor man doesn't die. He is finished off [by poverty]. (Rwandan proverb)

THE HEALTH SYSTEM in Rwanda is built around a network of 34 hospitals and 188 health centres. It provides the country with a much denser network of services than many others in Africa. Eight people in ten live within five kilometres of some sort of health facility. Of these health centres and dispensaries, almost half are run by non-governmental church organisations, most of them Catholic. The government helps to provide staff for these centres, and lays down policies to be followed. Currently it is trying to increase the amount that the 'consumers' (i.e. patients) are expected to pay for health-care, thereby reducing the burden of health expenditure on the State.

Who pays?

UNICEF is promoting the 'Bamako Initiative', under which medicines are supplied as donations to the health service, which then sells them to the newly created community pharmacies, which are under the joint control of the communes, the health centres, and the populations that they serve. The original intention of the Bamako Initiative, conceived by UNICEF at a meeting in Bamako, Mali, in 1987, was that sales of medicines should provide a profit to subsidise the operating costs of the health services. Currently Rwanda's aim is more modest: it seeks to ensure a regular supply of medicines to the health centres, where for years the free supplies from the government have not been enough to meet their true needs.

The health centres themselves are supposed to cover their running costs out of the consultation fees that they charge. Various kinds of health-insurance scheme, run on a community basis, are supposed to help people to pay the fees. In the case of those who are classed as indigent, local staff at the health centres are allowed to use their discretion to decide whether or not to exempt them from payment. Nevertheless the recent worsening in the terms of trade between the value of crops produced for export and the price of imported items, such as medicines, means that the number of people unable to afford health care has increased. The effect of this was seen in numerous health centres throughout Rwanda immediately after the devaluation of 1990, when receipts dropped dramatically and some health centres and hospitals were no longer able to pay their staff.

Those deprived of access, by distance or by poverty, to the 'modern' health sector have two choices. Either they use local traditional healers (some of whom are excellent, but many of whom can offer no real help) — or they simply suffer at home and hope that the illness will cure itself. When these strategies fail, such people often end up at the health centre in an advanced stage of sickness that is all the more difficult to treat because of the delay.

Who is responsible?

Rwanda's system of health care, based on treatment at hospitals and health centres, has reinforced the concept of ill-health as being an essentially medical problem, to be dealt with by the 'experts', rather than as something that is the responsibility of the whole community. Within this context the use of community health workers was actually banned for many years, despite

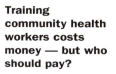

VINCENT BANABAKINTU/OXFAM

the attempts of some non-governmental organisations to promote it. This situation is now changing rapidly as the government tries to decentralise its structures, including health services. Its introduction of increased charges for consultations and medicines has been made politically acceptable only by involving members of the community on committees to supervise the use of the revenues generated.

The onward march of malaria ...

If the health care structures of Rwanda are different from many other sub-Saharan countries because of the density of the population, the diseases that they have to deal with are remarkably similar. For women the most important causes of illness are problems related to pregnancy and child birth. The most important causes of death for both men and women are malaria, respiratory diseases, intestinal diseases and, in urban areas, AIDS.

The incidence of malaria has been

growing rapidly over the past ten years. No one is quite sure of the reason. Some say it is due to a gradual increase in minimum night-time temperatures, allowing the mosquitoes that carry the disease to survive at higher altitudes. Others say it is due to the disease's increased resistance to medicines. Another theory suggests that it is because of the settlement of lands at lower altitudes, where malaria is endemic, and the increased travel (on improved roads) between these areas and the home areas of the migrants. Whatever the exact cause, the effect has been a dramatic increase in deaths from malaria, particularly in areas that were previously unaffected by the disease, where people had almost no resistance to it.

... and the advent of AIDS

A major new disease affecting Rwanda is AIDS. After an initial period of denying the problem, the Rwandan government moved quickly to establish an AIDS-control programme throughout the country. Nevertheless the rates of infection with the AIDS virus among the sexually active adult population rose between 1986 and 1990 from 18 per cent to about 33 per cent in urban areas, and from 2 per cent to 5 per cent in rural areas.[32] The National Aids Control Programme has estimated that the numbers of people who are HIV-positive in towns is growing at between 3 per cent and 6 per cent per year. The disruption caused by the war, and the forced return of almost 40,000 of Kigali's population to their communes of origin, will both have tended to increase the rates of infection (sero-conversion, as it is called) in rural areas throughout the country.

'Accept your brother with AIDS': a health education poster in Kigali

N'UWANDUYE SIDA NI UMUVANDIMWE

Ntumutererane.

PROGRAMME NATIONAL DE LUTTE CONTRE LE SIDA

B.P. 84
KIGALI.

Téléphone: 76309
73153

Even though AIDS has become the major cause of death in Kigali, its extent is often hidden by the fact that sufferers actually die of the opportunistic diseases that follow from the suppression of the immune system. rather than from one cause that can be called AIDS. In Rwanda, as elsewhere, AIDS carries a social stigma which prevents open discussion of the problem, even though it is becoming increasingly visible as people apparently in the prime of life suddenly die.

In the absence of any medical cure, what can be done to control the spread of AIDS? Researchers and health education workers are considering how people's personal behaviour might be altered. Despite a national programme of education about AIDS, sexual behaviour is a deeply personal subject in Rwandan society, as elsewhere, and changes in sexual behaviour are therefore occurring only slowly.

The full impact of the disease and the devastation that it will cause is not fully appreciated in Rwanda, any more than in most countries. It is a disease that particularly attacks men and women who should be at the peak of their productive capacity. The effects on the stability of society and the quality of its leaders, politicians, administrators, and entrepreneurs are incalculable at present, but probably they will be extremely damaging. A recent study[33] suggested that already 4,600 children in Kigali have been orphaned by AIDS, and that by 1995 the number could reach 160,000.

Despite the efforts of the Rwandan government and its people, the combined effects of the worsening terms of trade, declining food production, and the increasing insistence on 'cost recovery' in the health sector are likely to mean that the World Health Organisation's goal of 'Health for All by the Year 2000' is not met, and that the quality of service will tend to get worse rather than better.

Education: a cash crop to cultivate

I N AN AGRICULTURAL SOCIETY like Rwanda, suffering from a chronic shortage of land and a soaring population, education represents a vital route out of poverty — if only it is relevant and affordable. Rwandan people value education. One farmer recently described it as 'the only cash crop worth cultivating'.

Formal education in Rwanda is less than 100 years old: it was introduced by missionaries in 1900. Until Independence its main purpose was to provide catechists for the Catholic church and administrators for the government. Because the colonialists ruled indirectly via the Batutsi monarchy, the training of administrators was, in some schools, restricted to the elite of the Batutsi community.

At Independence in 1962 the country's new leaders appreciated the importance of education. But the need was great —

the vast majority of the population had never received any education at all — and resources were very limited. The problem then, as now, was how to provide everyone with adequate schooling, or how, in the government's words, to 'democratise' education.

In 1977 it was decided to make primary education more 'appropriate' by extending it from six to eight years, and to use the two extra years to teach practical farming skills. In addition, training was to be provided by Centres for Integrated Rural and Technical Training, the CERAIs, which were intended to provide pre-professional training for primary-school leavers who were not going to continue to secondary school. Accompanying this reform was a quota system, designed to ensure an ethnic and regional balance in the numbers of students entering secondary education.

VINCENT BANABAKINTU/OXFAM

A singing lesson at Gaseke School, Mbogo Commune

Education represents a vital route out of poverty

By 1990 the government was spending 22 per cent of its 'ordinary' budget (the resources that it raised nationally) on primary education. The results of this investment were disappointing. The ethnic and regional quotas did not convince people that the system was working fairly, while the extra two years of primary education seemed to be achieving very little, at great extra cost. The technical training provided by the CERAIs was not enough to make their students employable, and parents were more and more reluctant to send their children to them.

For the small number who managed to complete their secondary education there were problems too. The government's programme of structural adjustment had reduced the opportunities for employment in the civil service. But the education provided by the secondary schools was not equipping students with skills that were useful outside public service. Education was no longer the guaranteed passport to a better life that it once was.

Although 60 per cent of children attend primary school, just six per cent go on to secondary education, and fewer than one per cent to either the National University or to university abroad. Rwandan education, expensive as it is to the national budget, has fallen between the two stools of quality and scope. At present, neither adequate nor democratic, it is failing to meet the needs of the thousands of young people who join the working population each year.

Rwanda cannot afford to educate its people — but it cannot afford *not* to, either. The economy will suffer in the future from the lack of qualified people. For the vast majority of the population, who are not related to the country's existing elite, education is effectively beyond their means: one more survival strategy is effectively closed off to those who need it most.

Women's lives — signs of change

THE IMPACT of the economic and environmental crisis in Rwanda is hitting women particularly hard in their roles as mothers, farmers, and providers of wood and water. At the same time, their dynamism and their determination to change their situation is increasingly visible.[34]

Women as farmers

In Rwanda, 97 per cent of all economically active women are farmers, responsible for feeding their families and running almost all aspects of the household. The table opposite gives a rough guide to the roles of men and women in rural areas.

About a third of agricultural work is done jointly by men and women, so the breakdown of tasks is not as clear-cut as it looks in the table. Buying food for the family, providing health care, and paying school fees are also shared responsibilities. Men spend more time on non-farming work, which brings in a bit of extra money, such as brick-making, carpentry, and handcrafts. This is one of several tasks, such as building and land clearing, that are occasional in nature. In contrast, many of the women's responsibilities, such as child care and housework, are regular and continual.

The fact that they share certain roles leads many men to contest the fact that women do more work, but research suggests that women do 54 per cent of all agricultural work, and on average have 20 per cent less free time than men.

Despite their major role in farming, at least 38 per cent of women have never had any contact with a government agricultural extension agent, which perhaps explains why the extension services have failed to convince farmers to adopt farming techniques that could improve Rwandan agriculture.

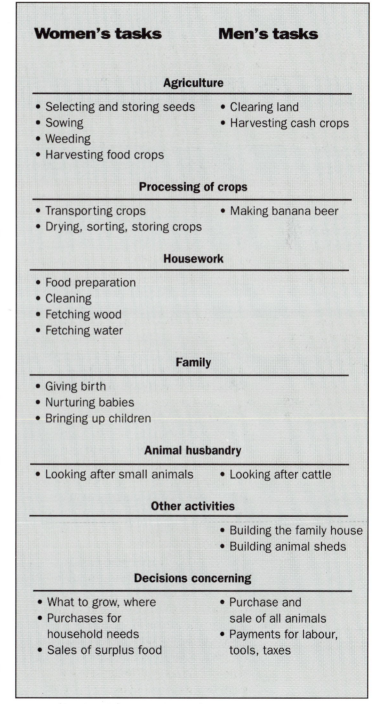

Women's tasks	Men's tasks
Agriculture	
• Selecting and storing seeds	• Clearing land
• Sowing	• Harvesting cash crops
• Weeding	
• Harvesting food crops	
Processing of crops	
• Transporting crops	• Making banana beer
• Drying, sorting, storing crops	
Housework	
• Food preparation	
• Cleaning	
• Fetching wood	
• Fetching water	
Family	
• Giving birth	
• Nurturing babies	
• Bringing up children	
Animal husbandry	
• Looking after small animals	• Looking after cattle
Other activities	
	• Building the family house
	• Building animal sheds
Decisions concerning	
• What to grow, where	• Purchase and sale of all animals
• Purchases for household needs	• Payments for labour, tools, taxes
• Sales of surplus food	

> Nta wumara imbuto mu nzu afite umukobga. — The household's seeds never run out if you have a daughter. (Girls are provident by nature.) (Rwandan proverb)

Women as mothers

Statistically speaking, the average woman in Rwanda gives birth to 6.2 live children during her lifetime. Even in urban areas, medical services are very limited. The complications associated with pregnancy and child-birth together constitute the biggest single cause of illness among adult women. For the 35 per cent of women who give birth at home without medical support, other than help from a traditional midwife, the situation is likely to be even worse. Clearly the family-planning programme of ONAPO is not only a means of limiting population, but also a means to improve women's health.

Another factor that undermines women's health is malnutrition. Between the ages of 0 and 5 years old, 32 per cent of girls are moderately malnourished, compared with 23 per cent of boys; the figures for severe malnourishment are 8 per cent and 4.7 per cent respectively.[35] Such malnutrition serves to handicap many women throughout their lives.

Women and the law

The legal position of women in Rwanda is ambiguous: the constitution declares that all citizens are equal, while at the same time accepting the validity of traditional law (which is patently unequal in its effects on men and women) in areas where there is no written code. This includes the question of inheritance. In addition, certain provisions of the civil code, such as the penalties that attach to adultery, discriminate against women.

The main problem for women is that the law does not consider them to be legally 'competent', and it recognises the man as the head of the household. A woman can acquire land by settlement from her parents, or by inheritance if she has no brothers, but this land becomes part of her husband's property and, if the marriage ends in divorce, she cannot claim it. If her husband dies, a wife inherits nothing. She may still use the family property if she has children, who are the actual heirs. In effect, a woman can own nothing legally — neither house, tools, livestock, nor crops.

This lack of legal status causes particular problems in the 22 per cent of households that are headed by single women:[36] widows, divorcées, single mothers, wives of migrant workers, and women who, like Marie-Rose Kabageni, have been abandoned with their children by husbands who have literally run away from their responsibilities. Although such women have a *de facto* independence (which they use to feed their families on average better than male-headed households), they also have even heavier work loads and no legal protection against any form of harassment.

In towns, and in the monetary sector of the economy, a woman's legal incapacity means that she can't open a bank account without the permission of the husband. This, combined with her inability to own assets, makes it almost impossible for her to obtain any credit from a bank. In 1989 the Banques Populaires (Peasants' Banks) gave just six per cent of their loans to women or women's groups.

Employment and education

In the area of government and the administration there were no women ministers until the coalition government of 1992. Nor were there any women *prefets* or *bourgmestres* (communal administrators). Only 7 per cent of positions of responsibility within government are held by women.

When children first enrol for primary school, the number of girls and boys is almost equal; but, as the years go by, it is the girls who drop out, or are withdrawn by their parents, rather than the boys. As a result, the number of girls in secondary and university education is far lower than that of boys. Part of the reason for this is that a woman's role is largely defined in terms of her eventual marriage. Many girls who do go into secondary education are provided with a three-year course in home economics that is of no use on the employment market, and only prepares them for their role as wives.

The strength of the social pressure to marry is witnessed by the fact that only one in 200 women will reach the age of 50 without marrying. But men and women are getting married later (24.5 and 21 years respectively), because of the rising cost of the dowry (usually one cow) that the groom must provide for the bride's family, and because of the shortage of land which makes it increasingly difficult to set up a new household.

Only 44 per cent of marriages are legally recognised. For the other 56 per cent the woman is vulnerable if the man leaves her, because, if he does not recognise the children as his, the woman will be obliged to look after them without help of any kind.

The story of Annie Mukankwaya

Annie Mukankwaya was born in Kibuye. She studied the 'home economics' course for three years in secondary school. On leaving school, she worked at a health centre run by Catholic nuns and lived with her parents in Kibuye. At the age of 26, unmarried, Annie became pregnant. The child's father denied any responsibility for the pregnancy or for Annie's problems. The nuns at the health centre dismissed her for immoral conduct and her parents sent her away, because they believed that an illegitimate child would bring bad luck, death, and disease to their farm and its livestock.

Annie went to Kigali with her baby and stayed with her sister while she looked for a job — without success, so her sister threw her out too. She left to look for shelter, and (as she put it) 'I met a man who agreed to help me and give me some money'. She rented a room for about £8.00 a month and had to accept the 'help' of other men (in return for sex) in order to survive.

Eventually she met a soldier from her home village who agreed to pay her rent. He was single, but refused to marry her

until he was sure she was still fertile. Unable to get pregnant, Annie went to the doctor for fertility drugs. When they didn't work, the doctor suggested that she bring her partner to be examined, but he refused. Unable to prove her fertility, Annie risks being abandoned again, and will have to survive on her wits as she did before. Her parents allow her to visit them, but still won't let her return to Kibuye to live with them. Annie's brothers won't look after her son, now six years old, because he would be a potential beneficiary of their parents' land.

Annie lives in an area of Kigali where 33 per cent of the adult population is HIV-positive. When asked about the threat of AIDS, she remarked, 'It is better to die of AIDS in two years' time than watch your child starve to death today.'

Annie's kinyarwandan name, Mukankwaya, means 'someone with courage'. Like many others surviving on the margins of Kigali, she is going to need all that courage during the remaining years of her life.

Getting organised

Women in Rwanda are increasingly conscious of the injustice of their position, and increasingly intent on changing it. Associations of women working together in rural areas grew in strength throughout the 1980s. Within these structures women have acquired a *de facto* legal status with

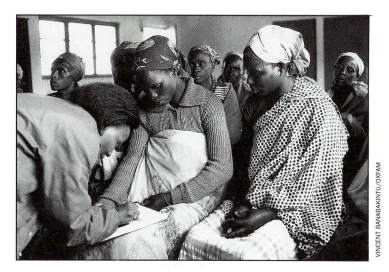

The Abashakamata Co-operative in Mutura Commune: one of hundreds of women's groups recently established in Rwanda

VINCENT BANABAKINTU/OXFAM

which they can gain access to land and credit. The associations also give women the increased self-confidence that comes from sharing their problems with each other, and being treated more seriously by outside agencies such as the communes and aid agencies.

Since 1984 IWACU, a co-operative centre for training and research, has been giving specific support to women's groups. Its first objective was simply to prove that women are just as capable as men in running associations, and especially in managing money. It also had to prove that women could benefit from training (even though they brought their babies with them), if their needs were considered from the start. At the same time the women themselves were starting to understand the nature of their marginalisation, and were gradually coming together in ever-larger federations which were able to start addressing the wider problems that faced them.

This strategy of working through associations has not been without its problems. Meetings take time — which women often do not have. The very poorest women in society almost never join such associations. Husbands are often reluctant to let their wives take part in such activities; many women give their husbands much of their earnings from the group, to persuade them to let them participate. The financial returns in proportion to the time invested are often so meagre that probably the only reason why the women remain involved at all is the intangible benefits of experience and confidence that they receive.

These grassroots associations of women are slowly developing a base from which the mass of Rwandan women may eventually be emancipated. Supporting this evolution are national institutions, which are themselves gathering strength. In the political arena the former single party created a women's wing called URAMA. Networks have also grown up within the Protestant churches and among women working in development projects of all sorts throughout the country. The latter has provided useful information and lobbying that has helped professional women to escape the isolation that they tended to feel in a male-dominated working environment. Several associations with a particular focus on the rights of women and children have been formed recently.

In 1992 a revised code of family law was passed, recognising a woman's right to use (but not own) her husband's property after his death, and to inherit family property — but only if she never marries or if, divorced or widowed, she returns home to live with her parents. However, it remains to be seen if these new rights will be applied in practice. It seems likely that women will have to lay claim to them actively, through their new networks and associations.

Women's groups help their members to develop skills and self-confidence: here Félicité Kandama gives her opinion during a village meeting

On the edge of the abyss

Prospects for prosperity

As we have seen, ordinary men and women in Rwanda are remarkable for their resourcefulness. But increasingly the typical smallholder with less than one hectare of land is slipping backwards through a ratchet of poverty from which there is little possibility of escape: if a member of the family falls ill ... or crops are diseased ... or the rains are too heavy or too scarce ... or if the farmer's animals stray on to someone else's plot and cause damage that the owner must pay for ... or if any one of a hundred other personal disasters occurs, the family's savings — perhaps reserved to buy a goat or cow or chickens — will have to be sold to pay for medicines, or food, or a fine. The children remain uneducated, and lose their chance of escaping the constraints of the agricultural life; or their parents gamble everything by selling land to pay school fees and buy books. If the child then fails the exams, or fails to find a job, the family is left destitute, with neither the rich relation that they had hoped for, nor the land that had hitherto supported them.

Farmers in Rwanda have worked hard to follow the various injunctions and instructions of the experts, intended to improve their agricultural performance. After 30 years of this, their position has scarcely changed, and recriminations abound. The 'experts' fail to appreciate that things would be even worse if it were not for the efforts of the peasant farmers. The finger of blame is pointed at everyone and everything: the government ... the researchers ... the extension agents ... the aid donors large and small ... the climate ... the structure of the world economic system ... the colonial legacy ... the churches ... the various political parties … even God himself! Each can make out a case in its own defence; each is probably partly to blame. The sad fact is that, despite the impression given by the opposition parties and the World Bank and other major donors, there are no easy solutions, no universal panaceas waiting to be discovered. Multi-party 'democracy' and economic liberalisation are not magic wands that will make the country's problems disappear.

So what is Rwanda's future? In the past, straight-line extrapolations of trends have failed to predict the future, and will probably do so again. Rwandan society is changing, and the changes in the different sectors interact to produce new changes, with new trends and new possibilities. The most encouraging aspect of Rwanda now is that fundamental changes are occurring in rural communities, which are beginning to form their own grassroots development groups. Rural men and women are starting to think about the sort of society that they want, and making their views known with increasing confidence. Both local politicians and outside aid agencies with their expert advisers will have to learn to listen to those views and learn how to respond to them. In an economic situation as desperate as Rwanda's, the only hope for a stable future will come from involving ordinary people in first defining the nation's problems, and then selecting the policies to be followed.

Prospects for peace

Sadly recent years have seen this fragile dynamic gravely threatened by a civil war in which politicians of all shades have been prepared to sacrifice the lives of the Rwandan population, the hard-earned gains of the past, the potential earnings of the future, and the emerging possibility of a freer society in their bids for political and military power.

Rwandan society is now more violently divided against itself than at any time since Independence. The war has caused incalculable damage to the economy and environment, and much needs to be done to encourage people to work together to heal the wounds of sectarian hatred. The peace agreement being negotiated in Arusha as this book goes to press will, if concluded, be a significant achievement, but no substitute for the process of national reconciliation that must now take place between ordinary Rwandans, if their country is to have a future. Until the genie of communal violence is returned to its bottle, much of the discussion in this book about alternative policies will be irrelevant. Rwanda stands on the brink of an uncharted abyss of anarchy and violence, and there are all too many historical, ethnic, economic, and political pressures that are likely to push it over the edge. Rwandans, and their political leaders inside and outside the country, are faced with a choice which will decide whether their country has any hope of a future.

The responsibilities of the rich world

Assuming that this most depressing of scenarios is avoided, the industrialised nations of the North must consider their responsibility for Rwanda's plight. Many Rwandans feel that their poverty is due to the structure of the world's economic and political systems, which permits prosperity in the North at the expense of poor countries like Rwanda in the South. As agencies like the World Bank and the Paris Club of creditors consolidate their collective power over poor countries, without any mechanism for accountability, we should not be surprised if countries in the South eventually start asking such questions aloud.

In the light of a world order which appears, from the perspective of Rwanda, designed to further the interests of people in the developed world, we in the North will be asked whether there is such a thing as a common humanity among all people. If there is, what does it mean in the practical terms of our mutual responsibilities? As the developed countries insist on sacrifices from poor countries, like Rwanda, to preserve the environment, to liberalise their economies and their trade, and to submit to the discipline of institutions that are effectively controlled by the developed countries, are we prepared to compensate people for those sacrifices, pay for the environment preserved in our name, open our economies to exports from the poor countries, and make our institutions accountable to those whom their actions affect?

Rwanda is on the brink: first its own people and then the international community must decide what sort of future it will have. If there is such a thing as common humanity, then the future of this small country in central Africa is indeed of concern to us all.

Storm clouds gather over the Nyungwe Forest

SU HOPKINS/OXFAM

Notes

1   René Lemarchand: *Rwanda and Burundi*, Pall Mall Press, London 1970, p.73.

2   Helen Codere: *The Biography of an African Society: Rwanda 1900-1960* (Institut National de Recherche Scientifique, Butare, Publications No. 12, p.199).

3   Cathy Watson: *Exile from Rwanda* (US Committee for Refugees, 1990), p.6.

4   'Profil socio-economique de la femme Rwandaise', Service d'Appui à la Cooperation Canadienne, Kigali, 1991, p.56.

5   Fédération Internationale des Droits de l'Homme: 'Commission Internationale d'Enquete sur les Violations des Droits de l'Homme Commises au Rwanda depuis le 1er octobre 1990' (Paris, March 1993).

6   Tharcisse Gatwa: 'Refugiés: un probleme incontournable', *Dialogue* 151, 1992.

7   'Enquete Nationale Agricole 1989', *Publication DSA No. 22*, Division des Statistiques Agricoles, Ministère de l'Agriculture, de l'Elevage et des Forets, Kigali, 1991 pp. 30-33.

8   'Première séminaire nationale sur la fertilisation des sols au Rwanda', Ministère de l'Agriculture, de l'Elevage et des Forets, Kigali, 1985, p.60, quoted in 'Le probleme demographique au Rwanda et le cadre de sa solution', Vol.I, Office National de la Population, Kigali, 1990, p.87. See also 'Enquete Nationale Agricole 1989', op. cit.

9   Material for this story was obtained from 'Les Retombées de la Famine', Bureau Social Urbain, Kigali, 1989.

10   Louise Sperling: 'Soil Fertility Management: Preliminary Notes', 1990, unpublished.

11   Service des Enquetes et des Statistiques Agricoles, 1986 (quoted in Commission Nationale d'Agriculture, Vol.I, Republique Rwandaise, Kigali, 1990, p.68).

12   'Situation Analysis of Children and Women in Rwanda', UNICEF, Kigali, 1988, p.70.

13   Commission Nationale d'Agriculture, Vol.V, République Rwandaise, Kigali, 1991, p.4.

14   In 1991 the imperatives of multi-party politics obliged the Government to increase prices slightly, despite continuing falls in the world price.

15   Commission Nationale d'Agriculture and OCIR: 'Café: 25 ans d'activités et perspectives', Rwanda, 1990.

16   'Document Cadre de Politique Economique et Financière à Moyen Terme', République Rwandaise, Kigali, 1990, p.1.

17   'Document Preparatoire à la Table Ronde des Bailleurs de Fonds', Ministère du Plan, Kigali, 1991, p.25.

18   IMF: International Financial Statistics quoted in *Country Profile 1991-92, Rwanda* (Economist Intelligence Unit).

19   *UN Handbook of International Trade and Development Statistics 1989* (New York, 1990).

20   'Memorandum sur la Politique Economique ...', op. cit.

21   'Retombées du Programme d'Ajustement Structurel', *Cahiers du Bureau Social* 83, Kigali, 1991.

22   *Change for the Better: Global Change and Economic Development*, Commonwealth Secretariat, London, 1991.

23   According to the preliminary results of the 1991 census, published in December 1992.

24   Because valley-bottom land remains Government land, farmers are allowed to use it, but not to own it. But it is an important addition to the area under cultivation.

25   ONAPO figures quoted in Commission Nationale d'Agriculture, Vol. IV, p.95, 1991.

26   ibid, p. 89.

27   See 'La Problematique de Rwandais Refoulés de Tanzanie', produced jointly by the Ministry of the Interior, ACORD, and Oxfam (UK/I), 1991.

28   N. Minot: 'Economie rurale rwandaise' in *Dialogue* 134, 1989, p.41.

29   The 1978 census and the Demographic Health Survey of 1983 suggested an annual growth rate of 3.7%. Preliminary results of the 1991 census, however, found a lower population than expected. The experts are now investigating the discrepancy. While the result is important for planning purposes, it does not change the fact of rapid population growth.

30   See 'Lettre Pastorale sur la Parente Responsable', issued by the Catholic bishops of Rwanda in November 1987.

31   *Dialogue* No. 129, 1988.

32   1986 figures from the HIV survey conducted by National Aids Programme during that year. 1991 figures are estimates.

33   'Quel Avenir pour les Orphelins de Malades du SIDA?', *Cahiers du Bureau Social Urbain*, No. 86, 1991.

34   This chapter is based on 'La role de la femme dans l'agriculture rwandaise', produced by the Division des Statistiques Agricoles of the Ministry of Agriculture, Kigali, 1990. 35 Moderate malnutrition is defined as a weight-for-age ratio less than 80% of that considered normal for children in a control population. Severe malnutrition is defined as a ratio less than 65% of the same norm.

36   Enquete Nationale Agricole, 1984.

37   Figures taken from Watson, op.cit., estimated on the basis of birth rates, death rates, and migration since 1962. A pre-Independence survey which judged everyone who owned more than 15 cows to be Batutsi gave rise to the unreliable (but frequently quoted) population figures of 1% Batwa, 15% Batutsi, and 84% Bahutu.

Facts and figures about Rwanda

Area:	26,338 sq km (for comparison: Wales: 20,766 sq km; Belgium: 31,000 sq km)
Population:	7.15 million (according to preliminary findings of 1991 census)
Population growth rate:	3.1% (preliminary findings of 1991 census)
Population density:	271 people per sq km, the highest in mainland Africa (Wales: 139, Belgium: 322)
Life expectancy at birth:	1991: 48 years for men, 51 years for women (UK: 72 for men, 78 for women)
Under-five mortality rate:	198 per 1,000 live births (UK: 11 per 1,000)
Number of doctors:	1 per 26,135 inhabitants (UK: 1 per 650, Belgium: 1 per 343)
Average no. of pregnancies:	6.2 per woman
HIV infection among adults:	18% in urban areas, 2% in rural areas (1986); 33% in urban areas, 5% in rural areas (1992 estimates)
Literacy:	Women 37%, men 64%
Ethnic groups:	Batwa 1%, Batutsi 9%, Bahutu 90% [37]
Languages:	Kinyarwanda (100% of population); French (used for central administration by less than 5%); Swahili (among traders)
Religions:	Catholic 85%, Protestant 14%, Muslim 1%. Traditional religion honoured Imana, the supreme creator of the universe; respect for ancestral spirits is still strong.
Capital:	Kigali (pop. 233,000)
Currency:	Rwandan franc (RWF)
Exchange rate:	At November 1990 US$1 = 71 RWF At December 1992: US$1 = 146 RWF
Gross National Product:	US$270 per capita (1992)
Main exports:	coffee 80% (£100m in 1986; £61m in 1987); tea 15%
Main imports:	petroleum, industrial products
Main food crops:	bananas (for cooking and for beer), beans, sweet potatoes, potatoes, cassava, sorghum (for beer)
Administrative structure:	Rwanda is divided into 11 regions (*Préfectures*) each with a *Prefet* (Prefect), appointed by the President. The préfectures are divided into sub-préfectures and then into 143 communes, each headed by a *bourgmestre* (administrator), also appointed by the President.

Postscript

This book was first published in July 1993. It ended with a prophecy: 'Rwanda stands on the brink of an uncharted abyss of anarchy and violence, and there are all too many historical, ethnic, economic, and political pressures that are likely to push it over the edge.' On 6 April in the following year, Rwanda descended into that abyss. One hundred days later, one tenth of the population was dead and two million people had fled from their homes. How and why did it happen? Which way now for Rwanda, in the hands of new leaders?

Genocide

The peace agreement which was negotiated in Arusha, Tanzania, to end the civil war that had destabilised Rwanda since 1990 was finally signed by President Juvenal Habyarimana in August 1993. (See pages 4–14 for the background to the civil war.) The Arusha Accords paved the way for power-sharing with internal opposition parties and with the armed Rwandese Patriotic Front (RPF), representing opposition groups in exile. But the Accords were never implemented. Those in power, particularly Hutu hardliners from the north, were even more resistant to sharing power with the minority Tutsi population after Burundi's Hutu President, elected in June 1993 (see p. 17), was assassinated by his own Tutsi-dominated army a few months later. The level of political assassinations, organised violence, and extremist rhetoric rose steadily in Rwanda through late 1993 and early 1994. Many observers, including the UN troops deployed in Rwanda to oversee the implementation of the Arusha Accords, reported the systematic training and arming of militia groups, known as *interahamwe* ('those who work together'), attached to extremist Hutu

political movements. But all the warning signs were ignored by the international community.

On 6 April 1994, the President's plane crashed near the airport in Kigali, killing Habyarimana and his Burundian counterpart. The authors of the assassination have

Churches became slaughterhouses during the weeks of genocide in April and May 1994
ROBERT MALETTA/OXFAM

Refugees cross the border into Zaire from Cyangugu Prefecture
HOWARD DAVIES/OXFAM

young men, mobilised by extremists, using farm implements as well as guns and grenades. Women and children, the sick and elderly, as well as men, were killed. The killers violated every traditional sanctuary, turning churches into slaughterhouses and hospitals into morgues. As neighbour turned against neighbour and teachers, doctors, and religious leaders, both women and men, joined in the slaughter, the very foundations of Rwandan society were destroyed.

The start of the genocide in April 1994 prompted the Tutsi-dominated RPF to advance its army from the north across Rwanda. The government and its armed forces, soldiers and militia, fled before this advance, encouraging (and in some cases forcing) ordinary Hutus to flee with them. Between April and July, about two million Rwandans fled to neighbouring Tanzania, Zaire, Burundi, and Uganda.

Although some 300,000 of those who fled in 1994 have now returned, about 1.7 million Rwandans still live in over-crowded and unviable refugee camps: there are an estimated 725,000 in North Kivu (Zaire); 280,000 in South Kivu (Zaire); 520,000 in Tanzania; and 100,000 in Burundi. The number of refugees now returning to Rwanda is easily out-stripped by the birth rate in the camps.

As the RPF advanced, and the government and its forces retreated, many Rwandans fled from their homes and ended up in camps for internally displaced people (IDPs). Those camps in the north-east, behind the RPF lines, emptied rapidly as soon as the RPF took Kigali and established a new government; but camps remained in the south-west, sheltering some 200,000 people, until as late as April 1995. Most of these people were Hutus, but there were small camps of surviving Tutsis.

It is reasonable to say that between April and August 1994 most Rwandan families either lost members in acts of genocide, or participated in such acts, or witnessed them. Most experienced some sort of displacement — either temporarily, in IDP camps, or more permanently

never been identified, but in Rwanda the event signalled the immediate start of a carefully planned and highly organised attempt to exterminate the Tutsi population, along with political opponents of Habyarimana's regime, Hutu as well as Tutsi. Within hours of the plane crash, armed militia, gendarmes, and soldiers had begun an orgy of slaughter which rapidly spread to the rest of the country.

Eighty per cent of the estimated 800,000 people who died (including 30–40,000 Hutus) were killed in the first six weeks of violence; they were mostly killed by outside the country. The people who bore the brunt of this tragedy were women and children. Today, about 70 per cent of households in Rwanda are headed by women, and one third to one half of women in the worst-affected areas are widows. Many women were raped during the genocide. The crisis left behind about 114,000 unaccompanied children. Many very young children could not survive when their families were killed or fled. Those Tutsis who did survive bear, in addition to their grief, a burden of guilt about their survival; they consider themselves to be the 'walking dead'. The social foundations of Rwanda have been undermined by fear, hostility, and insecurity.

There is no single, simple reason to explain what happened. This book describes the build-up of economic and political pressures. Their effects were compounded by a highly authoritarian national tradition, dating back to pre-colonial days. Government propaganda was extremely effective in convincing ordinary Rwandans that the RPF was synonymous with the Tutsi, and that therefore all Tutsi were military targets. Most killers were ordinary peasants. When orders came from government officials to eliminate the 'enemy', they obeyed, believing they must defend members of their social group against the Tutsi. Stories of individual heroism and self-sacrifice are frequent, but sadly insignificant compared with the vast numbers of people who, willingly or under threat, killed people whom they knew.

Reconstruction

The RPF won the civil war when they took Kigali on 4 July 1994 and formed a government of National Reconciliation, which included ministers from all political parties except the former ruling party; the Prime Minister and President were both Hutus. The government confirmed its willingness to work in the spirit of the Arusha Accords and committed itself to 'guarantee political pluralism and respect for individual and

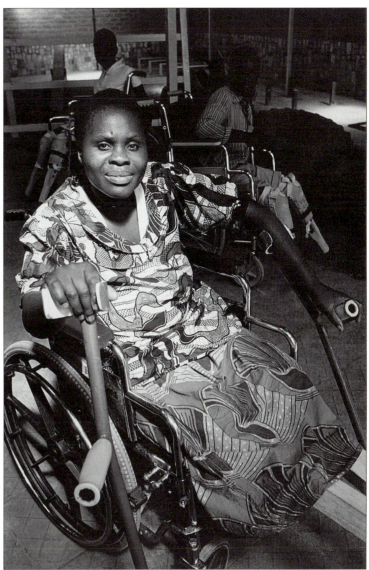

JENNY MATTHEWS/OXFAM

collective rights and liberties within a state subject to the rule of law'.

The government's desire was to return Rwanda to some sort of normality. Given that it found itself, in July 1994, with no functioning civil service, local government, judiciary or police, and given sometimes difficult relations with international donors, the government has achieved some notable successes in its efforts to rebuild the country. Much of the health service is functioning at pre-war levels; vaccine stocks and systems are rehabilitated; much work has been done to repair water and sanitation systems; and AIDS programmes are

'During the war I lost my husband and three of my four children. My brothers were killed and my home was destroyed. I stepped on a landmine on 7 October 1994. Now I am waiting for artificial limbs to be made. Then I will learn to walk again.'
Caritas Kayigawa, Kigali

again receiving some support (vital, given the country's pre-war levels of HIV infection, which can only have been increased by mass movements of people, widespread rape, and social disruption). Many primary schools reopened in September 1994; 1,000 schools had been rehabilitated and 120,000 textbooks provided by autumn 1995. Agriculture has received support through the distribution of seeds and tools, reaching over 50 per cent of farmers in the first season and 80 per cent in the second. A lot of work has been done to help unaccompanied children, although only about 10,000 have been reunited with their families. Local government staff are in place down to commune level.

The new government, lacking experienced managers and technical and professional personnel, could not efficiently apply large quantities of external aid. The international community was suspicious of the new regime in the early months and withheld vital supplies, so making it impossible for the government to prove its credibility. The government found itself in a vicious circle: money and training were not forthcoming and programme planning was weak — which reinforced donors' reluctance to provide funds.

Only in January 1995 did donors show their support for the new regime by pledging US$587m towards the government's Programme of National Reconciliation and Socio-Economic Rehabilitation and Recovery. But by the end of 1995 only one half of the pledges had been disbursed. Much reconstruction work is being carried out by UN agencies and non-government organisations (NGOs), which attract most of the aid disbursements and many civil servants, who leave their government jobs for better salaries. This has created resentment within the government, which expelled 40 NGOs in December 1995, mainly as a political act to try to reassert national sovereignty — although it is true that a few of the 150 NGOs present in Rwanda had been reluctant to coordinate their efforts with government ministries. These expulsions have not improved the government's relations with donors.

The government has committed itself to continue economic reforms agreed under the Structural Adjustment Programme signed in late 1990 (see pp. 33–34). However, further loans from the World Bank were not available until debts already incurred under the old regime were cleared, and this did not happen

A primary school in Kigali, 1995: most schools damaged during the conflict have now reopened

ADRIAN ARBIB/OXFAM

until the end of 1994. Since then, the World Bank has reopened its local mission and, along with the IMF, is in discussion with the government over its economic plans. Despite a relatively good start in economic management, there has been a frustrating delay in the rate of disbursement of World Bank credits.

The limited progress in reconstruction is due not only to scarce resources, both human and material, but also to the fact that many officials are inexperienced in government, and do not know Rwanda or understand it (having lived all their adult lives as refugees outside Rwanda). On the other hand, the majority of the country's inhabitants, who are Hutus, do not trust the government. The creation of a functioning and democratic State apparatus represents a challenge that will take time, resources, and political will to achieve.

Is reconciliation possible?

As part of the return to normality, internally displaced people were encouraged to go home, and eventually the remaining IDP camps were forcibly closed by the army in April 1995. The brutality of these closures did little to enhance the government's reputation abroad. But it also revealed internal divisions within the government, and the increasing dominance of hardliners. By mid-1995, many moderate Hutus, including the Prime Minister, had been sacked or had resigned and left the country. The period from May to July 1995 saw increased 'tutsification' and militarisation of government processes, and a reshuffle of the cabinet in August 1995 removed the four ministers most likely to criticise the government. The coalition government was broken.

The increasingly uncompromising attitude of the government in the first half of 1995 corresponded with the greatest threat of invasion from the former government troops and extremist militias. Although threat of a large-scale re-invasion has faded for the time being, extremists continue to mount guerrilla attacks across the borders, mainly from

the west. These seemed aimed at creating fear and insecurity in Rwanda and pushing the government to mount a counter-insurgency campaign and violate human rights, thereby undermining its international credibility. If civil war broke out again, the impact on Rwanda's development prospects would be devastating. It is vital for the future of Rwanda, and for stability in the region, that governments of neighbouring countries abide by agreements recently made during meetings in Cairo and Tunis, to stop the supply of arms, to put an end to military training on their territories, and to prevent the use of their territories as bases for incursions into Rwanda.

After July 1994, in response to the victory of the Tutsi-dominated RPF, thousands of Tutsi refugees who had left Rwanda in the 1960s and earlier began to return home (although many of them had never really known the country). Most of them came from Uganda and Burundi, but others from Zaire and Tanzania, and

Downtown Kigali: a mute witness of civil war
SIMON NORFOLK/OXFAM

67

even Europe. To date, about 800,000 have returned — a strange correlation with the numbers killed in the genocide. These returnees occupy large tracts of previously protected land which the government has opened up, or have taken over the property and land of previous inhabitants, who are either dead or living in refugee camps.

Refugees who fled from Rwanda in 1994 are deeply reluctant to return. In the early days, in the grip of former government leaders and their propaganda, they were afraid to return, despite the official government line that they would be welcome. Perhaps as many as 30,000 were directly involved in the genocide, and most are related to individuals who took part, and so are regarded as guilty by association. They fear, if they return, that they will be denounced and imprisoned or summarily executed by soldiers or relatives of those who were killed; they suspect that their land and property is occupied by other people and they fear further conflict. They also risk a real danger of being beaten or killed by elements within the refugee camps who seek to discourage voluntary repatriation. All these fears are fuelled by stories and rumours circulating in the camps. Reprisal killings in Rwanda did take place, mainly at the hands of soldiers and particularly between July and December 1994; perhaps as many as 100,000 people, both those who stayed and returnees from the camps, have died since the RPF came to power.

The government is divided on the issue of repatriation. Members of the government who want refugees to return consider that they represent a serious threat to stability while they are massed in camps on the borders, and that control of them will be easier inside the country. Others argue that the country cannot cope with mass return and the prospect of revenge killings and the conflicts that would inevitably ensue over property rights. It is probably true that a swift large-scale repatriation would plunge the country into a new cycle of killing and violence.

Although the international community responded with very large amounts of aid to the refugees, supplies are now drying up, and there is growing concern that the refugees will be forced to return to Rwanda — not only because of dwindling resources, but because host governments and populations have become increasingly hostile to the impact of refugees on their economies and environments. Several attempts have been made in North Kivu to encourage refugees to return, by surrounding the camps with soldiers. But only a few thousand people have gone back. Threats from within the camps and fears about what may happen to them in Rwanda are still strong enough to prevent voluntary return.

The need for justice

Without justice there can be no hope of reconciliation or reconstruction of Rwandan society. This has been the call of the government since taking power: the culture of impunity that has characterised Rwandan society for many years must come to an end. On 8 November 1994, UN Security Council members, in belated recognition of their obligation to 'prevent and punish genocide' under the Genocide Convention, established an International Tribunal. Judge Goldstone of South Africa was appointed as Prosecutor. But the Tribunal's progress has been painfully slow, and it was only in January 1996 that the first indictments were served against eight alleged instigators of the genocide. The first trials, of three high-ranking Hutu officials, finally began in May 1996 in Arusha. The international community's slow progress towards punishing the authors of the genocide, starting with the detention and extradition of its planners and leaders, has increasingly alienated the Rwandan government and convinced it that the world is indifferent to the genocide.

Internally, the judiciary needed to be rebuilt, as most judges, prosecutors, and police were dead or had fled. This too has proved to be a frustratingly slow process, while the prisons have filled up with people arrested on suspicion of genocide. There are now 60–70,000 prisoners, crowded into prisons meant to hold one fifth of that number; many deaths have resulted. Recodification of laws, preparation of dossiers, and training of personnel all take time, but there is also evidence of a lack of political will on the part of some hardliners in the government to see any trials take place which might find Hutus innocent.

It is clearly impossible to punish all suspects, so at a conference in November 1995 in Kigali, the government agreed in principle to a stratification of penalties according to different levels of guilt: the planners and leaders of the genocide must face the death penalty; those less guilty could benefit from plea bargaining; and at a lower level, others would be dealt with by traditional systems of justice, requiring them to recompense the families of the victims.

The return of the refugees, both 'old' (pre-1994) and 'new', is another area where justice is crucial. Many returned 'old' refugees are now occupying the homes and lands of 'new' refugees. Many of these farmers are squatters; the distribution of seeds and tools, and the passage of time, may encourage them to think that the land is theirs. Resolving conflicts over land-tenure rights is crucial to the successful reintegration of different groups.

The people who have been largely forgotten, by government and donors, are the survivors, who carry the double burden of grief and guilt. They are sometimes despised by newly arrived Tutsis, who suspect them of collaborating with the killers. Female survivors are in a particularly difficult position, given that they have no legal right to inherit property owned by their husbands or fathers (see pp. 55–8). There is an urgent need to reform the code of family law in favour of women, to give them some security and help them to re-build their lives. Little attention has been paid by outsiders to the psycho-social healing that must happen in the whole of Rwandan society, but particularly as it concerns

Kigali Prison, 1995: thousands of prisoners, suspected of complicity in acts of genocide, still await trial
JENNY MATTHEWS/OXFAM

women survivors, many of whom were raped, and most of whom have lost several, if not all, members of their families.

The failure of the UN in Rwanda

In the immediate aftermath of the genocide and before it had ended, the United Nations Security Council voted to reduce its forces in Rwanda to a mere token presence, on the grounds that the peace agreement which they were there to oversee was no longer valid. Although this decision was reversed in late May

A UN soldier from Zambia, patrolling Kibeho Camp
ADRIAN ARBIB/OXFAM

1994, it was a decision that cost many thousands of lives; a new UN force did not arrive in Rwanda until late August 1994, much too late to prevent the killings. While failing to prevent genocide and help the new government to consolidate its hold on power, the international community poured millions of dollars into refugee-relief programmes in neighbouring countries: US$1.4 billion was allocated to such work between April and December 1994.

It is widely acknowledged that the member states of the UN Security Council failed the people of Rwanda: they failed to heed the warning signs of impending genocide; they failed to react promptly and appropriately once the killing started; and they failed to intervene to prevent abuses of human rights in the period after the RPF came to power. In March 1996, on the invitation of the Rwandan government, the UN peace-keeping presence in Rwanda came to an end.

Which way now?

The long-term future for Rwanda will depend on the vision of its leaders, the rebuilding of Rwanda's distinctive social, cultural, and economic institutions, and regional alignments and interests. Recent initiatives have encouraged the governments in the region to work together to find regional solutions, and there are some signs of progress, which must continue to be supported by the international community.

There were already some two million Rwandese economic migrants and refugees outside Rwanda before the war, and it seems unlikely that the resource base in Rwanda can ever support the full return of all refugees. Refugees must continue to be encouraged to return, but provision has to be made for others to settle elsewhere in the region. Meanwhile, the situation in Burundi is deteriorating fast, and it is feared that large-scale civil war will result in yet further mass movements of people across borders. The international community must strive hard to learn the lessons from Rwanda and prevent the conflict in Burundi from further destabilising the region.

For the Rwandan government, the biggest problem is justice: until justice is seen to be done, the survivors will feel that they have been betrayed again. Until genocide is acknowledged by the perpetrators, trials begin, and prisons start to empty, there is little hope that well-meaning regional political compromises will be accepted by Kigali. There is a serious risk that the Rwandan government will become increasingly isolated and inflexible. Sustained and appropriate aid will do much to reduce this risk and contribute to the rebuilding of the country. The greatest danger is that the world is starting to forget.

Sarah Westcott
(Former Regional Manager of Oxfam's programme in Central Africa)
May 1996

Further reading

Destexhe, Alain: *Rwanda and Genocide in the Twentieth Century*, London: Pluto Press, 1995

Eriksson, John et al.: *The International Response to Conflict and Genocide: Lessons from the Rwanda Experience*, Copenhagen: Steering Committee of the Joint Evaluation of Emergency Assistance to Rwanda, 1996

Fegley, Randall: *Rwanda*, World Bibliographical Series, Oxford: Clio, 1993

Hilsum, Lindsey: 'Where is Kigali?', *Granta*, September 1995

Keane, Fergal: *Season of Blood: A Rwandan Journey*, London: Viking, 1995

Lemarchand, René: *Rwanda and Burundi*, London: Pall Mall Press, 1970

Mackintosh, Anne: 'International aid and the media', *Contemporary Politics*, Volume 2, Number 1, Spring 1996

Omaar, Rakiya: *Rwanda: Death, Despair and Defiance*, London, African Rights, 1994

Prunier, Gerard: *The Rwanda Crisis 1959–1994. History of a Genocide*, London: Hurst and Company, 1995

Vassall-Adams, Guy: *Rwanda: An Agenda for International Action*, Oxford: Oxfam (UK and Ireland), 1994

PHOTO: ANNE MACKINTOSH/OXFAM

Acknowledgements

Many people supported me while I wrote this book, and I thank them all, especially Oxfam colleagues in Kigali and Oxford, and those who commented on the text: Fiona l'Arbalestier, Emmanuel Bahigiki, Cindy Carlson, Dr Christopher Grundmann, Frans van Hoof, Josepha Kanzayire, Gesche Karrenbrock, Dr Katherine Krasovec, Joan Larosa, Ephrem Mbugulize, Veneranda Nzambazamariya, Father P. de Schaetzen, Louise Sperling, and Cathy Watson. Special thanks are due to people in Rwanda who told their stories to me; their accounts appear, mostly under fictitious names, in the text. Despite this help, I remain solely responsible for any errors of fact and interpretation.

David Waller
Kampala, Uganda
May 1993

Oxfam in Rwanda

Oxfam (United Kingdom and Ireland) has funded projects in Rwanda since the 1960s, and opened its own office in Kigali in 1979. Much of Oxfam's programme supported the emergence of Rwandan non-governmental organisations (NGOs), ranging from peasant farmers' associations to larger vocational training institutions.

Immediately after 6 April 1994, we lost touch with most of our Rwandan colleagues, as European staff were evacuated and communications collapsed. Over the ensuing months, members of staff and their families gradually reappeared, either in Uganda, where they had managed to escape behind RPF lines, or in Goma, Zaire, with the huge exodus of refugees in early July. Of a total of 30 Rwandans working for Oxfam in April 1994, two were lost during the genocide. The personal losses that some members of staff suffered are beyond comprehension: one lost at least 35 members of her family, including her husband, although she and her children survived.

Following work in IDP camps in the north-east between May and July 1994, the Oxfam office in Kigali was reopened in August, and some members of staff returned to their posts. We have re-built our programme on the principle of working in a way that seeks to bridge the gaps between different groups and to minimise further conflict. In the south-west of the country, an area likely to receive a large number of returnees, we run a programme to rehabilitate water systems, working alongside local community organisations. In the north-east we are helping to open up new areas for resettlement, in order to minimise future conflict between new and old refugees over land. In the south-east we are working with old and new communities in the health and water sectors. Our staff are trained to be prepared for emergencies, in order to be ready to respond if the situation deteriorates.

We are trying to work in a way that will increase openness between government and international NGOs and promote a suitable climate of trust for the re-emergence of local NGOs, so that we can reduce our operational presence and assume our more usual role of funding and advice, with the aim of strengthening local institutions. Oxfam also conducts a programme of research and advocacy, not only within Rwanda and in Africa, but also on an international scale.

Oxfam port-a-rig in action, drilling a borehole in Rwinkwavu (Kibungo Prefecture) to supply water to refugees returning from Uganda
PETER CRAWFORD/OXFAM